INTO THE HEART OF FAITH

TEN STEPS ON THE JOURNEY

DENNIS BILLY, C.Ss.R.

Liguori
LIGUORI, MISSOURI

TO MY NIECES,
ELIZABETH AND MICHELLE,
AS THEY BEGIN THEIR WALK

We walk by faith, not by sight.
(2 Cor 5:7)

Published by Liguori Publications
Liguori, Missouri
http://www.liguori.org

Library of Congress Cataloging-in-Publication Data

Billy, Dennis J.
    Into the heart of faith : ten steps on the journey / Dennis J. Billy.—
1st edition.
        p.   cm.
    ISBN 0-7648-0336-0
    1. Faith Development. I. Title
BT771.2.B52 1999
234′.23—dc21   98-35068

Scriptural citations are taken from the *New Revised Standard Version Bible*. Copyright © 1989 by the Division of Christian Education of the National Council of the Churches of Christ in the United States of America. Used by permission.

CONTENTS

INTRODUCTION

*H*ave you ever observed little children trying to learn how to walk? It takes a long time for them to get the hang of it, a very long time. No matter how often they fall forward, or backward, or sideways, or forward again, they will not give up until one day they succeed, first, at standing up straight and maintaining their balance, then at taking one hesitant step, then a second, a third, and so on, until they are able to walk about at will without even thinking about what they are doing.

Learning how to walk is an exceedingly difficult and, at times, even dangerous task. It is a skill that most of us learned long, long ago—so long ago, in fact, that we may now even take it entirely for granted. Just imagine what your life would be like if you never had learned how to walk or if, through some tragic set of circumstances, that precious skill was now taken from you for life. Even the simplest of life's daily tasks would suddenly become difficult (for example, getting dressed, going down the stairs, crossing the street, and so on). You would be confined to bed, or to crutches, or to a wheelchair and would have to depend on others for things that you formerly could have done for yourself. Not being able to walk certainly would take some getting used to, and the adjustment, no doubt, would take its toll on other areas of your life.

WALKING BY FAITH

Walking, to my mind, is a very apt metaphor for faith. With faith, we are able to set out each day on a new leg of our spiritual journey. Without it, we can do nothing but shift about aimlessly in the lonely interior regions of the soul. Even though faith itself is a gift from God and not something we acquire through our own efforts, it is we who are ultimately responsible for its growth (or its decline) in our lives—hence, the parallel with walking. Just as little children learn how to walk during a long, grueling process of trial and error, so too must we learn the difficult lessons of what it means to walk in faith, that is, to trust God moment by moment with the nitty-gritty details of our lives. Such lessons are not learned from books, but from experience. They do not teach us about God, but confer on us an experience of God. These lessons open our eyes to the possibility of a deep, intimate relationship with the God who is with us (Mt 1:23) and who calls us his friends (Jn 15:15).

Walking by faith is a basic necessity of the spiritual journey. If we are not prepared to trust God with the details of our lives, then it is useless to talk about our ultimate destination or any of our intermediate goals in life. Why talk about the places we plan to visit if we are not prepared for the inconveniences along the road? Why prepare our provisions for the journey if we know that we will never get past the first obstacle we face? Why talk about our final destination if we refuse to take the necessary steps to get there? To set out on a spiritual journey we need to have some basic survival skills in our pilgrim repertoire. Above all else, we must know what it means to walk in faith.

And just what does that knowledge entail? To walk by faith means that you and I are trying to foster our personal relationship with God. It means that Jesus Christ is a living, personal presence in our lives, a friend to be trusted, someone we can count on and turn to at any time and at any place, and especially when we are in need. It means that we seek guidance from him in the concrete circumstances of our lives: through prayer, through the Scriptures, through the sacraments, through the wise counsel of others. It means believing that Jesus is not only our friend, but also our traveling companion through life, that he is there beside us when we wake up in the morning, as we go about our daily activities, right up to the time when we go to bed. It means believing that there is not a single thing we do that Jesus does not do with us and offer us help with. It means having the eyes to see the active, personal hand of God in everything we do. It means living our lives in such a way so that we become more and more aware of the movement of the Spirit in our lives.

To walk by faith is to walk with Jesus, the man—not merely with his teachings, not merely with some idea of him, not merely with some image of him that we have formed in our minds—but the real McCoy, the person of Jesus *himself*! The more we walk by faith, the more we become aware of the active, living presence of Jesus in our lives. We walk with Jesus, and Jesus walks with us. Arm in arm, we set out on a journey that promises to be a first-class adventure for both of us—and all because we have taken the time and put in the effort to learn what it means to walk by faith.

LEARNING TO WALK

When children learn how to walk, they first have to acquire and then have to coordinate a number of different skills. They do so not merely through their own efforts, but with the help of others whom they imitate and look to for moral and other kinds of support. Where would they be without their mommies and daddies who hold them gently, let go of them at appropriate times, but who are there to catch them when they lose their balance? What would they do if there were no grownups of any sort to watch them, encourage them, and help them along?

When learning how to walk, children first need to strengthen their legs and learn how to stand by themselves without any artificial supports. This achievement requires that they learn to maintain their balance by using the muscles in their legs and torso as counterbalancing forces to prevent them from falling too far forward or backward or wherever their weight happens to be tending at the time. Once this simple skill of upright balance is mastered, they then need to focus on a direction and risk upsetting their balance by setting out for it first with one foot, then the next, and so on. The first steps children ever take are always the most difficult, for they must combine their newly learned skill of keeping their balance with the pressing rush of their forward momentum. The chances are that they will fall many times before they finally get the hang of it. Even then, they will continue to refine their newly learned skill until it becomes second nature to them. Just think of what children have to go through to take their first steps! They must keep their balance using different muscles as they move upward and downward, backward and forward, all in one continuous sweep. If they are not careful, they will slip, fall, and, if no one is there to catch them, perhaps even hurt themselves.

When learning to walk by faith, we must develop a similar set of skills that help us to keep our balance. We cannot develop these skills on our own, for they go far beyond our natural capacity. They ultimately derive from God, who offers them to us to use at our own discretion, when we see fit, and depending on our inclination to do so.

What might some of these skills entail? To walk by faith we need to be able to face our fears, to befriend our doubts, to embrace the suffering that comes our way. We need to work through painful memories, to break up our cold, stony hearts, and to foster intimate relationships with others. We need to forgive and to receive forgiveness, to reach out to others in love, and to make our deepest longings for God rise to the surface of our lives. We need to live in hope and to share that hope with those who have little to hope for. These are some of the basic skills involved in our walk of faith.

Because we must be ready to use these skills at any time, as the circumstances dictate, it is essential that they become deeply ingrained habits that come to the fore when needed even when we don't have time enough to think about the need to use them. Walking by faith means having that special combination of spiritual skills that enables us to keep our balance on our journey through life and to make those special adjustments that are necessary as the road narrows and turns and encounters rough terrain.

STEP BY STEP

This book looks at the separate, component skills that are necessary for the ongoing walk of faith. By focusing on a specific skill (for example, overcoming our fears, facing our doubts, dealing with suffering, and so on), you and I will be able to see how complex an activity walking in faith really is. We will also be able to appreciate the help offered to us by Jesus, our closest companion and friend, as well as all the love and support offered to us by the members of his Body.

The danger in looking at these aspects of the walk of faith individually is the tendency we may have to mistake any one of them for the walk itself when, in point of fact, each is but a single component of a vast network of skills that we, as believers, may be called upon to use at any particular moment. The focus here is not on the spiritual journey itself, or on the ability to walk in faith that is necessary for it, but on the very skills which make such walking possible. The more we understand these skills, the better will we be able to integrate them and use them when the need arises.

To help you get started, I have introduced each of the ten chapters of this book with an appropriate text from the Christian Tradition. The purpose of these quotations is to highlight the importance that the particular skill considered in that chapter has for the walk of faith. These skills deal respectively with

(1) facing our fears; (2) overcoming our doubts; (3) dealing with suffering; (4) healing our memories; (5) changing our hearts; (6) fostering intimacy; (7) seeking forgiveness; (8) serving the poor; (9) longing for God; and (10) living in hope. This list is merely representative and in no way exhausts all the possible skills and combination of skills needed in the walk of faith.

The goal of this book is to be suggestive of the necessary skills for our walk of faith rather than comprehensive. Those skills that have been left out can either be derived from those already treated or studied separately at the reader's own convenience.

The order in which the skills appear, while not essential to understanding the intrinsic connection of the skills to each other, has a logical progression of its own. Skills relating to difficulties in getting started on the walk of faith are treated first (chapters 1 through 4). Those skills relating to activities done during the walk of faith are treated next (chapters 5 through 8). Those relating to the destination of the walk of faith come last (chapters 9 and 10). The ten-step layout of the book, moreover, is not intended as an instruction manual for appropriating these skills. As stated earlier, these skills are gifts of God which become more deeply rooted in us through use. Reading about these skills will only get you so far. You learn how to walk not by reading about it, but by walking. The most a book like this can do is point out areas where your walk of faith might be improved.

To help you in this way, I have listed a number of reflection questions at the end of each chapter under the heading entitled, "Surveying Your Skills." These questions are meant to assist you in examining in detail the basic elements of your walk in faith. Some of you may find them helpful. Others may not. They are there for your own benefit, to be used when (and if) you need them. Some of you may find it helpful to write your *own* reflection questions that focus more on the details of your own particular walk. Others may wish to focus on only one of the questions provided. Still others may have your own way of looking at your daily faith experience. The point is not whether or not you use the questions as points of departure, but that you find the time to sit down and reflect upon your walk of faith. The questions appear at the end of each chapter to remind you of this important spiritual task.

YOUR BREATHING

Next there is the whole matter of breathing. Are you aware of how important your breathing is to the way you walk? You won't get very far if you try to walk while holding your breath. To get the most out of your legs you need to synchronize their movement with your breathing, that is, establish just the right rhythm between the steps you take and the rate of your inhaling and exhaling. Increase your pace, and you will naturally speed up your breathing. Slow it down, and you will breathe more slowly.

Something similar to this is true for our walk in faith. The various skills dealt with in the chapters of this book represent nothing more than the movement of our hips and legs. As necessary as they are for what we hope to do, they will not get us very far if they are not properly coordinated with the inhaling and exhaling of our spirits. Prayer does for the spirit what breathing does for the body: it keeps it vibrant and full of life. With it, we are fortified and strengthened for the road ahead; without it, we have little hope of making any real headway in the spiritual life. "The person who prays will certainly be saved."[1] Everything depends on whether we allow the Holy Spirit to breathe within us and enliven our hearts with a deep and endearing love for God.

One long and venerable tradition in Eastern Christianity actually draws a close connection between prayer with breathing. Known as the *hesychasm*, from the Greek word for "stillness" and made famous in such spiritual classics as the *Philokalia* and *The Way of the Pilgrim*, this approach takes seriously the apostle's injunction to "pray without ceasing" (1 Thess 5:17) by seeking to synchronize one's breathing and even the beating of one's heart with the words of the Jesus Prayer: "Lord, Jesus Christ, have mercy on me!" Its goal is to make these words a part of the fiber of one's being so that they permeate one's consciousness and enter into every activity of one's life. The beating of one's heart and the rhythm of one's inhaling and exhaling mark the pace at which these words ebb and flow in a person's conscious and unconscious thought. One inhales the first part of the Jesus Prayer and exhales with the second. This is done over and over again, thousands of times each day until the words seep down into a person's unconscious awareness. Eventually one gets to the point where the words become so much a part of a person's normal life processes that they cannot be separated. At that point, we are able to pray even as we sleep.

I have organized this book in a similar way. It opens with "Stillness," a short poem about the close connection between prayer and breathing, and closes with "Step by Step," a slightly longer poem about the ongoing walk of faith. The book's ten chapters or "steps" then fall between two pages devoted to prayers, one of which is entitled "Breathing In" and the other "Breathing Out." Each of these are two simple prayers to Jesus: one, for the gift of a wise and understanding heart; the other, for a request for companionship on the journey. Each prayer is made up of four simple phrases that can be prayed either separately or in their entirety, as you so desire.

There is nothing unique to these two opening and closing prayers, other than they are special to me. The first, I wrote many years ago for the prayer card distributed at my ordination and first Mass. The second came as I began to understand my life more and more in terms of a journey. Both have become important prayers in my life. They have accompanied me down through the years and, like the Jesus Prayer itself, have filtered down into some of the deepest parts of my soul. I have prayed them countless times down through the years and, I assure you, even during the writing of this book. I place them at the beginning and the end of the book not to impose them on you, or to highlight their literary value, or even to suggest that you pray them (although I can't see that hurting much). They are there because they have become so much a part of my own walk in faith, of my own inhaling and exhaling of the Spirit in prayer, that I cannot now justify my leaving them out. These words are mysteriously intertwined with the countless thousands of breaths that went into the writing of this book and are largely responsible for whatever life you receive from it. They are there primarily to serve as a reminder—both to you and to me—that we will go nowhere in the spiritual life (and certainly nowhere in our walk in faith) if prayer itself does not become a habitual and vibrant part of our daily lives.

Just what am I getting at with this digression? In one sense, nothing much; in another sense, all that really matters. I ask you to pray as you read this book. Pray what I have placed before you, if it moves you and you feel so inclined to it. Pray the Jesus Prayer, or one of its several variations. Pray your own short but fervent prayer—perhaps one that you yourself have composed. Use your imagination: "The Holy Spirit will teach you at that very hour what you ought to say" (Lk 12:12). What is important is not the words you choose, but that you do, in fact, pray. Breathe the words in and out. Experience the stillness in your heart. Let it accompany you as you move through the book from word to word, from sentence to sentence, from paragraph to paragraph. Let it carry you with your breathing as you turn the pages, as you move from chapter to chapter, from step to step. In doing so, you will get much more out of the book I now place before you, and you yourself will find new meaning in the phrase "spiritual reading."

CONCLUSION

Walking by faith is as much about prayer as it is about the skills involved in the walk itself—perhaps more so. It is my hope that this book will deepen your insight into both of these important aspects of your spiritual journey. I also hope that they will deepen your awareness of the close, intimate relationship that you are called to have with God. Walking by faith means walking with the Lord. We may not always be aware of the divine presence as we make our way through the more difficult stages of our journey. We may call many aspects of our faith into question and, at times, even wonder if God really cares for us. At times such as these, however, it is important for us to remember that Jesus' presence in our lives is not a function of our awareness of him. If that were the case, he would be present in the lives of only a handful of people, and our faith tells us that that simply is not so. Jesus, "God with us," is closer to us than many of us realize. When he seems absent, it may very well be that he is simply too close for us to recognize him.

Ultimately, this book is about a risk that each of us decides to take (or not to take) each day of our lives from the time we get up in the morning to the time we go to bed—and then some. That risk—"the great bet," as Pascal termed it—is whether we are to live our lives as though God existed and walks beside us, or not. We should try to be aware of the risk involved in this walk of faith. In doing so, we will recognize the existential dimension of the choices we make in life and be able to assess more readily the direction our lives have taken. We should also appreciate all the more the skills put at our disposal to help us along our spiritual journey. Without them, the going would be much more difficult than we could ever imagine.

It is now time for me to end this brief introduction and let you experience for yourselves what, up to this point, I have only been able to describe (and even that rather poorly). It is now time for you to depart my company and concentrate on the various tasks at hand. Be gentle and patient with yourself along the way. You learned how to walk once; you can do so again. In fact, if you have stayed with me this long, you have probably already had a good bit of practice at it. No matter. One can always benefit from going back over the basic skills that help us make our way through life. Besides, in a real sense, we are *all* beginners when it comes to walking in faith.

Weak and forgetful as we are, much of what we have already learned will need to be tested and confirmed again and again, every day, for the rest of our lives. Such is our human plight: most of us are slow, very slow, learners. So be patient with yourself as you embark on this process—as God is patient with you. Eventually, you will get the hang of it. Who knows? You may even surprise yourself! This much I assure you: Once you risk learning how to walk in faith, you will have quite an adventure ahead of you. From the first step to the last, I promise you won't regret it.

STILLNESS
(A Poem)

Sojourning with self
in silence,
communing with life
in death,
listening to around,
finding abound,
then taking another
breath…

BREATHING IN
(A Prayer)

Walk beside me, Lord.
Speak to my heart.
Enable me to listen.
Help me to understand.

1
FACING OUR FEARS

THE FIRST STEP

Let nothing disturb you,
Let nothing scare you,
All is fleeting,
God alone is unchanging.
Patience
Everything obtains.
Who possesses God
Nothing wants.
God alone suffices.

Teresa of Ávila,
Her Personal Bookmark[2]

hildren do not allow the fear of falling down to get
in the way of their desire to walk. If they did,
they would never get past their first failed attempts.
Much the same holds true for our learning to walk by faith. If
we wish to do so, we must overcome the fear of failure. We
have all experienced fear in our lives. If we examine ourselves
honestly, most of us could probably point to something we are
afraid of even now.

Fear is deeply personal. What makes one person afraid
may cause another to smile or possibly even laugh. Fear also
can be intensely social, embracing whole communities and, at
times, entire cultures. The fears that haunt us come in many

shapes and sizes. They can be great or small, distant or close, rational or irrational, conscious or unconscious, holy or profane. Whatever they are and however they present themselves, we can be sure that, just as with children who are learning to walk, we too are capable of looking beyond them.

THE COURAGE TO FEAR

Our fears pass in and out of our consciousness. They are most dangerous when they lurk out of sight, beneath our present awareness. Sometimes they stay submerged for long periods of time. It is then when they inflict their greatest damage. It is then when they cause us to act out of character, in ways we are often ashamed of. When our fears are "out of sight," they cause us to act "out of mind." When we are conscious of them, we can at least face them and devise ways of dealing with them constructively. Many of us are afraid of our fears and not even aware that we are living in fear of being afraid. This fear is perhaps the greatest one of all. It condemns us to a life of unreflective action, where we avoid rather than acknowledge, and hide from rather than seek out our deepest selves.

Although it takes courage to face our fears, it sometimes takes even greater courage to be afraid. Fear is a natural defense we have when we come face-to-face with imminent danger. It is an alarm system that tells us to be ready and on the alert. When trouble arrives, fear is often the most reasonable reaction we can have to the situation at hand.

When we are not afraid even though we should be, we are at a distinct disadvantage. In this instance, we have no way of assessing the various threats that we encounter in our journey: our guard is down; our nerves are dulled; our adrenaline is low. We cannot react at an optimum level to the dangers before us. As a result, we do not take the proper precautions. We attack and are overwhelmed; we move forward and are taken by surprise; we plunge ahead when retreat is the only reasonable course of action.

Fear is not inimical to bravery. A courageous person is someone who is afraid when danger calls, but who does not allow that fear to cause him or her to shirk the responsibilities of the moment. A coward, by way of contrast, is someone who, by not acknowledging his or her fears, either runs away from them or parades around displaying a false bravado.

Even when we *should* be afraid, however, we must be careful not to allow the emotion of fear to overwhelm us. We need to walk a delicate line between too little fear and too much. In the face of grave danger, too little fear makes us rash and quick to judge; too much fear, however, makes us spineless and lacking the necessary wherewithal to carry out our responsibilities to ourselves, to others, and to God.

How exactly do we achieve that balance between too little fear and too much fear? What can we do to integrate our fears constructively into our lives? In this case, experience is our great teacher. If we examine ourselves or ask men and women who, in our judgment, represent the epitome of bravery, we will find that most came to that balance by making mistakes and learning from them. Few people are born with such a balance already in place. Most of us have to come to it. Just as we learn to walk by trial and error, trying this way and that, falling first forward and then backward (and sometimes even sideways), we learn how to control the fear in our lives by reflecting on our past and learning from our mistakes. Once we realize that we have overreacted in one situation or underreacted in another, we are less likely to repeat the same mistake.

When we learn to tame our fears and befriend them, we can begin to understand the meaning of patience. Patience is having courage in the small nitty-gritty details of the moment. It means not running away from life, but embracing it with all of its foibles and difficulties, pains and hardships. Patience bears the suffering of the moment and refuses to let any obstacles, large or small, get in the way. A patient person is someone who has learned that the meaning of life is locked up in the present. By sticking with the present, by facing it head-on with no illusions or starry-eyed ideas of either the past or the future, the patient person embraces life with both feet planted firmly on the ground. This total embrace of life brings with it suffering and joy, relief and sadness. It enables a person to live both in and out of time in the midst of the most ordinary daily activities.

IRRATIONAL FEARS

Sometimes our fears are justifiable; sometimes, not. They can get out of hand and take control of our lives. They can paralyze us in the face of adversity and prevent us from leading normal lives. When our fears overwhelm us in this way, they become irrational. Since we are not able to see beyond them, they become obstacles to our growth.

How can we tell if we are the victims of irrational fears? What can we do to confront them? What can we do to change them? If we have a particular phobia in our lives, the chances are that we have tried our best to cater to it. We are afraid of heights, so we stay away from tall buildings. We are afraid of flying, so we never go on a plane. We are afraid of feeling closed in, so we stay away from crowded rooms and wear loose-fitting clothes. We are afraid of crossing the street, so we never go outside. The list can go on and on.

The problem with this approach is that we live around our fears without ever confronting them. We try to avoid all situations that will activate our fears and bring them to the fore. We fit our lives around our phobias and try as much as possible to pretend as though they do not exist. The trouble is we *know* that they do. We cannot fool ourselves. We cannot avoid all such situations. Sooner or later, we will find ourselves in the very circumstances we tried so hard to avoid. Since we never developed any healthy coping mechanisms to deal with our irrational fears, we become the prey of raw emotion and are made to go where we do not want to go.

This book is not the place to go into a detailed explanation of the cause of our irrational fears. That we will leave for the specialists to debate and decide. For our purposes, suffice it to say that our phobias (and we all have varying degrees of one kind or another) stem from an aspect of our early development that has somehow gone awry. If we wish to become whole, we must face our irrational fears head-on, that is, acknowledge that they exist, seek out appropriate help (professional or otherwise) that will help us cope with them, and live through them once they show their ugly heads on the horizons of our lives.

We will probably never get over completely the effects that such phobias have on our lives. We can, however, break their stranglehold on us and, with the proper support and coping mechanisms, be able to lead normal, productive lives. We will be able to get onto that plane, cross that street, walk into that crowded room—and take control of our lives. We were never meant to live *in* fear, least of all irrational ones. If we succumb to them, we will find that they will gradually encroach into more and more areas of our lives and become more and more numerous. "Then Jesus asked him, 'What is your name?' He replied, 'My name is Legion; for we are many'" (Mk 5:9).

BEYOND FEAR

If we face our fears, journey with them, talk to them, befriend them, we will eventually find that, one by one, each will depart of its own accord. "There is no fear in love, but perfect love casts out fear" (1 Jn 4:18).

Our fears accompany us on our journey through life, but

so does Christ, who is "God with us." As we draw closer and closer to Jesus, the man from Nazareth, the power our fears have over us will weaken and fade. To draw closer to him means to grow in the love of God. God's love for us and our love for God become deeply intertwined. Our relationship deepens in trust and bears the marks of a true and lasting friendship. God seeks our good, as we seek the good in God. We come together freely and share in a mutual relationship. We dwell in each other's hearts and carry the other with us wherever we go.

There is no room for fear in a deep, trusting relationship with God. Once we are convinced of God's unconditional love for us, all of life's trials, all of its dangers and obstacles dwindle in significance. "Who will separate us from the love of Christ? Will hardship, or distress, or persecution, or famine, or nakedness, or peril, or sword?" (Rom 8:35). Friendship with Christ gives us a courage that carries us beyond fear. That is not to say that we no longer have need of those healthy, rational fears that have become a necessary, indeed, vibrant part of our sojourn through life. It does mean, however, that the phobias that control us will loosen their hold on us and dwindle down to nothing as we journey more and more deeply into the mystery of God. Even our healthy fears are changed by virtue of our deepening relationship with Christ. We find our patience deepening and our ability to withstand the obstacles that come our way growing in ways we never before thought possible.

As our relationship to Christ deepens so does the way we perceive life. As it changes, so does our understanding of what really matters. The Apostle Paul gives expression to this deep spiritual experience: "In any and all circumstances I have learned the secret of being well-fed and of going hungry, of having plenty and of being in need. I can do all things through him who strengthens me" (Phil 4:12–13). With Christ at our side, there is nothing to fear. Not only can nothing separate us from his love; with him, we find within ourselves the strength to overcome even the harshest of life's difficulties, be it physical deprivation, emotional stress, mental strain, social disfavor, spiritual dryness, or what have you. Whatever we face, we face together as the closest of friends who seek nothing but the other's good. Christ's good becomes our good; our good, Christ's.

If this picture may seem just too good to be true, it may be because many of us have consistently settled for less for so much of our lives that we become suspicious of anything that offers us more of anything. Some of us, moreover, may have a difficulty in viewing Christ as someone who will lead us beyond our fears because it is he who, for whatever reason, has all along been the central object of our deepest fears. We cannot speak of a lasting friendship with Christ if we continue to view him as someone constantly monitoring our behavior, ready to use our faults and failings against us when we stand before him in judgment. We cannot believe in Christ's friendship if we allow our fear of him to get in the way and prevent us from trusting him with our lives.

There is, of course, a healthy fear of the Lord. This fear is rational and is rooted in a sense of awe at the great work which God has done for us in Christ. Fear of the Lord is a gift of the Holy Spirit. It enables us to reverence the greatness of God and makes us marvel all the more that God wishes to befriend the likes of us. If a healthy fear of the Lord does anything, it draws us closer to Christ and enables us to appreciate the friendship we have with him all the more. True friends come to know themselves in the life of the other. True fear of the Lord—not the irrational kind—helps us to see in the majesty of Christ our own magnanimity and nobility of soul. As a single soul existing in two bodies, we who fear the Lord look within ourselves and stand in awe before the promises of God and our own divine destiny.

BEHIND FEAR

To many of us, however, our destiny seems a very long way off. Believing as we do in the presence of Christ in our lives, we have to admit that there are times when he is difficult to see, when he seems to be not only distant but, at times, even absent from our lives. It is at those moments when we must be especially on guard. As Jesus himself reminds us: "When the unclean spirit has gone out of a person, it wanders through waterless regions looking for a resting place, but not finding any, it says, 'I will return to my house from which I came.' When it comes, it finds it swept and put in order. Then it goes and brings seven other spirits more evil than itself, and they enter in and dwell there; and the last state of that person is worse than the first" (Lk 11:24–26).

Behind every fear in our lives stands seven others that are far worse. Jesus wishes not only to exorcise our fears, but even the fears behind our fears. It is for this reason that, at various times in our journey through life, he seems to distance himself from us a little and seems to allow us to walk alone. At such times, we encounter fears we never knew we had. We look back on our lives and begin to second-guess ourselves. Unsettling questions lodge themselves in our ears. Have we gone too far? Have we underestimated our fears? Have we wasted our lives on an empty promise?

The fears in our lives are sometimes so deeply rooted that it takes the experience of God's absence to bring them to the fore. The fears behind our fears and the fears behind even those fears can be difficult to exorcise from our hearts. We cannot and should not try to do it by ourselves. These layers of fears are probably more than we can handle, and we run the risk of being overwhelmed by them. No, the appearance of these new fears within our hearts is a challenge for us to trust even more deeply in the power of the Lord to free us from our own inability to love. Only Jesus' perfect love is able to cast out our fears. When we do not experience his presence in our lives, we are called to believe nonetheless that he is there at our side, watching over us as we make our way through the dark in search of a safe footpath upon which to tread.

It is at times of challenge like these when we are able to peer beneath our fears and encounter what lies behind them that we are able to come face-to-face with the shadow side of our lives. Up until this point, we may have been able to escape this head-on confrontation with the darkness in our hearts. When we encounter the fears beneath our fears, however, we reach the limits of what we can do to exorcise the roots of fear in our lives. We now recognize that we can only go so far, that something more is required than merely opening up the windows and tidying up the room. Our fears and phobias can be so deeply rooted in our lives that we need to look to another for help. Should we seek professional assistance? Perhaps, but that decision is best left in the hands of competent judges. Whatever happens, we need to realize that, ultimately, our deepest fears can be exorcised by no solitary human hand, regardless of how well it is schooled in the arts of healing.

When we confront the fears beneath our fears, we can no longer pretend that what we see does not belong to us, as if it was a bad dream from which we one day would awake. When we look them in the eye, we cannot help but see the side of us that we are ashamed of and wish we could forget. We look at them and realize now, perhaps for the first time in our lives, that these fears will only dissipate once we journey with them and allow them to speak aloud in the daylight what previously they were only permitted to whisper in the darkest corners of our souls.

It is at this point that Jesus appears again on the scene (as if he ever left). He has allowed us to travel on our own so that we might encounter our deepest, most hidden fears, the ones so deep that it took a semblance of healing in our lives to rouse them from their slumber and wreak havoc in our lives.

Once we encounter and recognize our utter helplessness before them, he appears once again at our side to comfort us and to remind us that he is never far away from us and that he is constantly looking out for our welfare. He takes up his journey with us once again and promises to be with us until even these fears grow tired and fall somewhere by the wayside. We, for our part, are asked to do nothing but walk and pray in the company of our Lord. If we do this, we will learn the deeper meaning of trust in our lives, that part which accepts all things as coming from the hand of the Lord and which is able to believe that "all things work together for good" (Rom 8:28).

CONCLUSION

Fear is an unwelcome companion through life. We travel with it, but long to be rid of it. Even when fear is a necessary companion, we do not enjoy its company. Fear makes us feel weak and uneasy. More than any other emotion, it reminds us of our own imperfections and those of the world we live in. Something within us tells us that fear is foreign to us and makes us less than what we can be. We long to rise above it and call forth our greatest potential. We are afraid, however, of challenging our fears for fear of what they might do to us.

We all have had to struggle with fear. We know the uneasiness it brings to our lives. We also know how much we try to avoid it and wish it would simply go away and leave us alone. It would be a mistake, however, simply to lump all fears in the same category. Some are even necessary to our lives. Without them, we would not be well-equipped to deal with the real dangers that we come across in our sojourn through life.

It is our irrational fears—our phobias—that should concern us. We overcome them not by ignoring them, pretending they do not exist, or, worse yet, repressing them, but by confronting them, naming them, befriending them, journeying with them. Our fears can do nothing to us. It is our negative reactions to them that can harm and, at times, do great damage to us and others.

When we journey with our fears, both those which first present themselves to us as well as those which take a long time to surface and whose roots are deeply entrenched in our hearts, we find that they are not as daunting as we first made them out to be. Why is this so? Because another companion has joined us along the way. Jesus travels with us (Lk 24:15). In befriending us, he also befriends our fears. As our relationship deepens, we come to see that nothing can truly harm us when we are held in God's embrace. The more we trust God, the more do our fears loosen their hold on us. Eventually, we become so centered in our friendship with Christ that we will no longer advert to our fears and they themselves will gradually fade away.

We face our fears by first facing Christ and accepting his companionship in our travels through life. Throughout that journey he manifests himself to us in many ways: in our hearts, in our friends, in the Church, in the sacraments, in the Scriptures, in the events of the day, even in our enemies. If we are to face our fears by means of our friendship with Christ, we must ask for the ability to discern his face when and where he chooses to reveal it to us and not merely at our own convenience. The more we are able to discern the face of Christ in our lives, the easier will it be for us to trust him and reach out to him, especially in times of need.

It is Christ, the source of perfect love, who casts out our fears. He exorcises them by being our companion on our journey through life. With him by our side, our fears cannot overwhelm us. They may journey with us for a time, sometimes for years, perhaps even for most of our lives; but they cannot and will not conquer us. The time will come when they too will tire of the road we have chosen and fall by the wayside of their own accord. When they finally leave us, perhaps on that day we will come to see how all during our lives Jesus has been by our side, saying to us over and over again what he said so many years ago to his closest disciples: "It is I; do not be afraid!" (Mk 6:50).

SURVEYING YOUR SKILLS

1. Are you aware of your fears? Can you describe them? Can you distinguish the subtle differences between them? Can you tell how you feel when they come upon you? Are some more difficult to deal with than others?

2. How do you deal with your fears? Do you ignore them? Run away from them? Meet them head-on? Do any of them ever overwhelm you? Do they prevent you from functioning? Have you ever learned anything from them?

3. Have you ever tried to befriend you fears? Dialogue with them? Journey with them? Do you know what it is like to be brave and fearful at the same time? Have you ever had an experience where fear brought out the best in you? The worst in you?

4. Do you ever think of Jesus as being afraid? If so, how so? How do you picture Jesus in relation to your own fears? Does he understand them? Does he feel them? Does he help you to understand them? Does he help you to tame them?

5. Do you bring your fears to God in prayer? Do you share them openly or try to hide them? Do you place them in God's hands or try to handle them yourself? Do you believe that God can help you overcome your fears? Do you have any doubts about it?

2

OVERCOMING OUR DOUBTS

THE SECOND STEP

> There is so much unbelief in the world, for too many
> people speak of God unworthily and never stop find-
> ing fault with his activities in a manner they would
> not dare use toward the most incompetent work-
> man. What we really want to do is restrict his work
> so that it conforms to the rules and boundaries that
> our limited reason considers suitable. We try to
> improve and do nothing but complain and grumble.
>
> Jean-Pierre de Caussade,
> *Abandonment to Divine Providence*, II.6[3]

Children's first steps are always made in uncertainty.
They believe they can walk, but are not quite sure of
themselves. They stumble and fall until they get the
process of walking right. They eventually get the hang of it,
but expect to lose their footing at any moment. They do not
know what their next step will bring.

Our walk in faith is not all that different. We journey
through life with hesitant, uncertain steps. We believe, or at
least say we do, but take back our words many times each
day. We prefer ourselves to others. We fail to follow our deepest intuitions. We trust no one but ourselves, and even that we
find difficult to do. We second-guess our decisions and regret
lost opportunities. We are haunted by the past, evade the

present, and live in fear of the future. We believe in God, but only nominally, only when we find ourselves with no alternative, and even then with only a halfhearted assent.

The paths we travel are marked by doubt. Our steps are fragile and unsure. We walk with only a vague notion of where we are going—and why. Doubt accompanies us in everything we do. It is so close to us that we hardly recognize its presence. It is so near that we can barely distinguish it from the rest of our surroundings. We are defined by our doubts as much as by our beliefs—perhaps more. The faces of our doubts haunt us at every turn.

THE FACES OF DOUBT

What are these faces of doubt that accompany us on our journey? How can we recognize them? What do they say to us? Who or what are they moving us toward—or away from? Such questions bid us to examine some of our deepest attitudes and preconceptions about life. They ask us to examine ourselves with total candor. Only by confronting the faces of doubt in our lives will we be able to understand the truth about ourselves. Only by staring these faces in the eye will we be able to look beyond them and continue our journey in faith.

RATIONALITY AS A FACE OF DOUBT ~ To begin with, there is the *rational* face of doubt. This facade of rationality demands proof before giving assent and subjects everything to microscopic analysis. We in the West are quite familiar with what such detailed probing can do. In the last few centuries, we have spent much of our time and resources sharpening the blade of critical reason. Occam's razor and Descartes' enlightened *cogito* set off a series of philosophical and empirical investigations that have brought both great benefits and terrifying horrors to the world in which we live. Systematic doubt, the engine that powers this critical search for truth, has opened up new venues of human learning and technological advancement. Over the last few centuries, we have progressed in areas of scientific discovery never before dreamed of. Even greater developments seem to be in store for the future.

This methodical search for "clear and distinct" ideas, however, has not come without a price. Our fascination with critical reason has dimmed our awareness of other equally valid (albeit different) kinds of knowledge. We have become so enamored of the benefits wrought by the scientific method that we have fallen into the mistaken judgment that it is the sole measure of truth. We have so narrowed our understanding of authentic human knowledge that we have become blind to some of our most basic intuitions about the meaning and purpose of life. We have come to doubt everything that does not measure up to the strictest test of critical reason. Very few (if any) areas of our lives have been exempt from these claims. Those that *are* have been labeled "irrational" and unworthy of a dignified response.

The result of all this reliance on critical reasoning has been the gradual impoverishment of our souls. We who have mastered the exterior world have become increasingly out of touch with the interior reaches of the heart. We have relied so much on the powers of reason that we have nearly succeeded in separating our minds from our bodies, and our bodies from our hearts.

This lack of integration in our lives has overflowed into our religious outlook. The only viable options in a world-view supported solely by critical reason are the leap into the absurd or a leap into unbelief. All other responses are considered suspect or, at best, "unenlightened." All else is subject to doubt. Even now, with the waning of the modern era and the end of reason's stranglehold over human knowledge, the unsettling voices of doubt whisper in our ears and move us against our deepest hopes. We who have passed through the Enlightenment have lost our innocence and have no way back to the simpler, less sophisticated times of our ancestors. Doubt is here with us to stay. The choice before us is to befriend it or be ruled by it.

MISTRUST AS A FACE OF DOUBT ~ Doubt also can wear a face of *mistrust*. In this guise, doubt prevents us from entering into authentic human relationships. We are social, relational beings by nature. Trust is at the heart of all healthy human interaction: in friendship, in the family, in the local community, in society. Without trust, we isolate ourselves from others and live in a world marred by our own suspicion and incapacity to relate.

This kind of doubt can have disastrous effects on both ourselves and others. Our lack of trust often spawns a similar response in those around us. Hurt feeds upon hurt; anger upon anger. Negative feelings build and spiral out of control. Before we know it, we find ourselves living in an environment of loneliness and mutual suspicion, one which can easily lead to hatred and violent attacks on others. Whole societies can be infected by this rancorous animosity which can be manifested in a breakdown of dignified human relationships both within their society and in its affairs with others. This face of doubt thrives on fear. It instills those living in such an environment with a deep-rooted anxiety about the hurt others may inflict on them. Because they wish not to be harmed, they often try to inflict the first blow.

This mistrust of other people often spills over into our relationship with God. We refuse to trust in the divinity's ongoing love and concern for us. We cannot believe that God would take the time to look out for our own welfare. We do not believe in a God who desires to enter into a lasting covenantal relationship with us. Instead, we are afraid of what God may do to us. We try to hide our sins or pretend they do not exist. We relate to God only on the most superficial of levels, because we feel we would be punished or, worse yet, completely abandoned if we were never known as we really are. God, in the eyes of the dubious, mistrusts his people as much as his people mistrust God. That is why we are subjected to such exacting demands on us and why we will be judged accordingly. We secretly loathe God for acting in this way. We wish the divinity would rise above the petty mistrust and anxiety that mars our own relationship with others, but we refuse to allow it. We say we love God, but deep down inside we feel strongly otherwise. We disdain the very image in which we ourselves were created.

In the end, this face of doubt is rooted in our own self-loathing. We mistrust God and others because we cannot trust ourselves. We cannot trust ourselves because we secretly hate ourselves and spend most of our time and energy trying to convince ourselves otherwise. This lack of self-love comes from a poor self-image which itself can arise from many causes: a dysfunctional family environment, abusive parents or authority figures, exaggerated expectations placed on us by others. The list can go on and on. Its effect on us is a lack of interior peace and a corresponding lack of integration in our lives. We experience a void within ourselves, but do not know how to fill it. Only love can show us the way out of such isolation.

ACTIONS AS AN EXPRESSION OF DOUBT ~ There is, finally, the *performative* face of doubt. This face is the most difficult of the three to envisage and therefore the most elusive. For this reason, it is potentially the most destructive to the spiritual life. This side of doubt drives a wedge between our most dearly held beliefs and the actions that define our lives. It refuses to enflesh belief with action and, in so doing, creates a huge rift between the people we profess ourselves to be and the actions that mark our lives.

This kind of doubt is the most dangerous because we tend not recognize it as doubt at all. We have fashioned our lives in such a way that we exist in two very different worlds that have very little to do with each another: an interior world of consistently held beliefs; and an external world where these beliefs do not apply. This kind of doubt would be hypocrisy if we were aware of the discrepancy between faith and action.

It is precisely because we are *not* aware of the gap between belief and action, however, that makes this form of doubt so insidious and so difficult to root out. We need not be conscious of our doubts to suffer from their destructive influence in our lives. The dichotomy between the interior and exterior worlds often goes undetected. Sometimes, our belief system must be shaken to its foundations before we realize that we inhabit but a single world and that our actions are themselves the bearers of our most deeply held beliefs.

"For just as the body without the spirit is dead, so faith without works is also dead" (Jas 2:26). Those of us who live by performative doubt number among the walking dead. The tragedy of it all is that we think we believe one thing when our actions reveal our beliefs to be quite different. We profess our belief in a God of love, yet participate in societal structures of oppression that trap people in their poverty. We profess our belief in the dignity of all human beings, yet act in prejudicial ways toward others who do not share our same religion, race, nationality, or ideology. We say we love God, yet go about our daily lives motivated more out of self-interest than a desire to carry out his will. These are just some of the subtle ways in which performative doubt can make its devious way into our lives.

We are normally too unaware and too complacent to rid ourselves of performative doubt by ourselves alone. It usually takes some other person or some external event to shake us up and to help us to see that what we say we profess is not what we profess at all. Such a moment is an invitation to conversion, a call to lead more integrated lives by uniting our inner and outer worlds and allowing them to be permeated by a deep and living faith.[4]

BEFRIENDING OUR DOUBTS ∼ To prevent our doubts in whatever form they take from taking control of our lives, these doubts must be recognized, befriended, and brought along with us on the journey. This acknowledgement does not mean that we acquiesce to their destructive power or go where they wish to lead us; nor does it mean a refusal to change our attitudes or our way of living. It means only that we be honest with ourselves and accept ourselves as we are without illusion. We must accept the fact that most of us will be unable to change overnight such deeply embedded attitudes and ways of behavior. We must also accept the fact that we cannot make this change on our own, without any reference to God or to our neighbors.

Those of us who wish to overcome our doubts must recognize the deep hold they have on us and the way they have infiltrated some of the most fundamental aspects of our daily lives. We must also recognize that, in today's world, the faces of doubt are the constant companions of an understanding heart and that, in the long run, we will either be ruled by our doubts or allow them to join us on our journey of faith. In the latter case, they often provide us with occasions for deepening and enriching our faith.

What does using our doubts in a positive way mean in concrete terms? In the first place, it means differentiating our doubts and letting them come to light. We do this by examining our lives, often with the help of a spiritual director or seasoned, sympathetic counselor, and identifying as much as possible those areas where narrow-mindedness, fear, mistrust, and ignorance have power over us. This reframing of doubt into a positive force requires a good deal of time and patience, since we are often too close to what we are looking for.

Reflecting back on our dealings with other people, our intimate relationships (or lack thereof), our most deeply held beliefs (and prejudices), and our attempts at concerted action (or inaction) helps us to put some distance between ourselves and our lives as we have lived them up to the present. This distance enables us to encounter ourselves in a new and different light. We are able to see ourselves as others see us and, on occasion, even as God sees us. We are then able to put a face on the particular areas of doubt in our lives, to give those faces names, and welcome them as our companions.

Why is it so necessary to journey with our doubts? When we journey with our doubts we come to understand them better and, in doing so, come to a deeper knowledge of who we are. Those of us who do not befriend our doubts bury them inside ourselves where they wreak havoc in our souls and eventually in the lives of those we encounter. The only way to prevent such an outcome is to journey with our doubts so that we come to know them better. The more we come to know them, the easier will it be for us to deal with them and, ultimately, tame them. Once a doubt is tamed, it no longer poses a threat to our well-being. A domesticated doubt is no doubt at all, since it has been owned and integrated into our self-identity.

We know we have befriended our doubts when we find ourselves dialoguing with them rather than acting out of them, when we find out where they are coming from rather than where they are taking us. When we travel with our doubts in this honest and inquiring manner, we gradually find that they are not taking anything away from our faith, but are actually contributing to it. Faith is forged by God in the furnace of doubt. The person of deep faith is someone who has journeyed a long time with his or her doubts. By befriending them and traveling with them, we learn from them and come to appreciate their intimate connection to our faith.

BEYOND DOUBT

The faces of doubt in our lives, however, can accompany us only so far. Sooner or later, the time will come for us to move beyond them. Our faith will have become deepened because of them and we will be ready to let go of them. This process will take place with no sudden shock or fanfare. It will happen naturally, probably over a long period of time. One day we will be reflecting on something and notice that the doubts which used to trouble us so much in former times have long since receded to the background.

"Truly I tell you, unless you change and become like children, you will never enter the kingdom of heaven" (Mt 18:3). As we mature in our faith, we come to appreciate the simple things of life, and our faith becomes more and more like that of a small child. There is little room for doubt in a life that is being drawn increasingly closer and closer to God. This is so not because we are no longer capable of doubt, but because we no longer need to cling to the presumption of certitude. Our probing and inquiring minds stand in awe before the mystery of God. As we mature in faith, we become further and further steeped in that mystery, and there comes a point when close human scrutiny no longer makes any sense. At that point, all we can do is step back and allow God to be God in our lives. It takes the faith of a child for that to happen.

We sometimes forget that God accompanies us in our journey of faith. Jesus, "God with us," welcomes our doubts and is the one who transforms them. He is with us as we recognize them, befriend them, and travel with them. He is the one who encourages us to dialogue with them and to come to a deeper knowledge of ourselves through them. God, who uses all things for our good, permits our doubts in view of a much greater good: we would not appreciate our faith as much if we did not have to struggle for it; our journey to God would suffer from a lack of suffering and not be a measure of the true cost of discipleship.

Whatever they are, the faces of doubt in our lives ultimately reveal to us the mysterious face of God. They do so not because they have any intrinsic merit of their own, or because they themselves are capable of revealing the divine mystery, but because God takes us where we are and comes to us—doubts and all—in the circumstances in which he finds us. Since doubt, with all its faces, has become our constant companion in our journey through life, God has deemed to make of it a vehicle of self-revelation. Faith comes through hearing—as does doubt. "Let anyone with ears listen!" (Mt 11:15).

CONCLUSION

Our world is shaped as much by our doubts as by our faith—perhaps more. We should not fear our doubts, cast them aside, repress them, or treat them with suspicion; nor should we be intimidated by them or somehow think that they are too much for us to handle. Doubt, it is true, enters our lives because of a lack of faith. This lack provides the space in which doubt grows and flourishes. It also provides us with the opportunity to enrich our faith in ways never before imagined. Our doubts can help us to root out the false images of God that govern our lives and deepen our knowledge of self. They can also give us fresh insights about other people and the world in which we live. By conversing with them, we befriend them and gradually experience an invitation to deepen our faith in the living God of love who will never abandon us.

It is wrong to conclude, however, that the faces of doubt in our lives will *necessarily* deepen our faith. If we fail to befriend them and journey with them, we will find ourselves ruled by them and one day overwhelmed by them. To live in doubt is to live with risk: it can bring us to a deeper affirmation of life, but also it can bring us to an equally emphatic denial of it. The dark side of doubt can eat away at everything we hold sacred in life. If we are not careful, we will find that doubt will keep us from, rather than lead us to, the threshold of the holy.

In the end, what matters is not that we live in doubt (this is something we simply cannot avoid—at least in the present life), but *how* we live in it. *How* we live in doubt is a question closely connected to *how* we live in faith. In fact, we have here virtually two different ways of asking the same question. Doubt implies faith; without it, it would turn to unbelief. Each acknowledges the uncertainty of belief, but approaches it from a different perspective: one by way of affirmation; the other by way of questioning. This connection between doubt and faith fuels the torch that lights the path before us. It is just as important for us to understand our doubts as it is our faith. Doubt in search of understanding is another way of speaking of faith in search of the same, which is another word for theology or "God-talk."

The faces of doubt in our lives wish to be recognized, named, and addressed. They wish to be examined, understood, digested, and acted upon. They wish to share with us the story that has brought them to the fore of our consciousness. They wish also to journey with us, as a companion to faith, as far as the mysteries of faith will allow. When we allow this to happen, our doubts undergo an unusual transformation. The more we journey with them, the more they loosen their hold over us and allow us to attend to other, more urgent needs. The more we befriend them, the more we understand their origins in our own lives and in the lives of others. The more we converse with them, the more will they reveal to us the hidden treasures of God. The faces of doubt can (and often do) reveal to us the mysterious face of God. In this respect, conversing with our doubts is a natural and often necessary prelude to a life of prayer.

SURVEYING YOUR SKILLS

1. How do the faces of doubt manifest themselves in your life? Are some forms of doubt more prevalent than others? Have you ever felt as though your faith has been shaped by your doubts? Are faith and doubt for you contradictory or complementary responses to life?

2. What kind of doubts do you have? Do they relate to the intellect? To trust? To action? Which of these is more common to your experience? The least common? What do your doubts tell you about your faith? What do they tell you about the kind of person you are?

3. Do you ever feel as though you are walking more in doubt than in faith? If so, how would you describe the feeling? Has this experience deepened or weakened your faith? Has it opened your eyes or given you any new insights into yourself? To others? To God?

4. Have you ever had the experience of helping another person sort through his or her doubts? If so, what did that feel like to you? Did that experience help you in your own walk of faith? Did it make your walk of faith more difficult? Do you yourself turn to others to help you sort through your own doubts?

5. Do you bring your doubts to God in prayer? Can you tell Jesus your doubts? If not, why not? What do you think he would say about them? Do you think he understands? Can you picture Jesus ever having any doubts? Can you picture him ever walking in doubt? Hanging in doubt?

3
DEALING WITH SUFFERING

THE THIRD STEP

My son, what is it you say? Why do you thus complain? Cease, cease, complain no more. Consider
My Passion and the passion of My saints, and you
will see well that what you suffer for Me is very
little. You have not yet suffered to the shedding of
your blood, and surely you have suffered little in
comparison with those who have suffered so many
great things from Me in time past, and those who
have been so strongly tempted, so grievously
troubled and in so many ways put to the test. It
behooves you, therefore, to remember the great,
serious things others have suffered for Me, so that
you may the more lightly bear your little grief. And
if they do not seem little to you, take care that your
impatience is not the cause.

Thomas à Kempis,
The Imitation of Christ, III, 19[5]

*L*earning how to walk can be very painful. Not only
do children have to develop and strengthen the muscles
in their legs and lower body, but they also have to bear
the scratches and bruises that come from their unsuccessful
efforts. Those learning how to walk by faith must face similar
perils. Each of us knows what it means to suffer: some more

than others. Suffering is part of the human experience. It is so much a part of us that it is hard for us to envision what life without suffering would be like.

Although common to us all, suffering is also very personal. Each of us is unique in all the world; our suffering follows suit. Although we may be identically diagnosed, our illnesses are not the same when it comes to their internal effects on the psyche. Suffering is as much psychological as it is physical; it also has social and spiritual dimensions that must be factored in. These dimensions of human suffering manifest themselves in each of our lives in different combinations and in varying degrees. Although the suffering of Job resonates in each of our hearts, it was very much his own, something which made him feel very much alone in the world, abandoned by his family, his closest companions, even by God.

THE HUMAN SITUATION

The suffering we experience in our lives is a herald of the death that will one day come upon us. The way we react to it now is probably a good approximation of how we will respond to it in death. Suffering helps us to understand our limitations. Try as we may, we can never control it or overcome it; it is usually the other way around. Suffering makes our nerves raw and exposes them to the air. It unleashes life's primitive forces within us and washes us in emotions we never knew we had or have long since forgotten: sadness, anger, melancholy, rage—to name but a few.

Suffering forces us to face what we are all too willing to overlook in our lives. It brings us face-to-face with our broken, wounded natures. It pushes us into areas of human experience that most of us would otherwise be all too willing to avoid. It makes us ask questions about ourselves and the purpose of human existence that otherwise we would never probe and seek to fathom.

Why must I go through this? Why did this happen to me? Why would God allow this to happen? Why doesn't he answer my prayers? These and similar questions fill our minds when suffering suddenly forces its way into our lives. There is no need for us to define it or measure it, or philosophize about it. Each of us knows what suffering is and each of us has first-hand knowledge of it. Each of us has had to deal with the uninvited pain that finds its way into our lives. Each of us has found a way to cope—or not cope—with the human situation in which we find ourselves, where suffering is always waiting for us around the next bend of our journey.

REACTING TO SUFFERING

The way we react to the suffering that comes our way says a lot about who we are and the types of people we are in the process of becoming. There are at least six general types.

THE PARALYZED ∿ Some of us are so afraid of suffering that we have become paralyzed by our fears and shut ourselves up in an airtight, risk-free environment in an attempt to ward off or delay the inevitable. We retreat into ourselves and lock other people out of our lives because we are afraid of being hurt by them. We ask little of God in the hope that God will ask little of us. We end up leading sad, joyless lives since we never really set out on the human journey for which we were made. We also lead battered, self-defeating lives since, try as we may, we cannot lock ourselves away from our innermost fears and the impending approach of death.

THE OVERWHELMED ∿ On the other extreme, others of us have developed no coping mechanisms whatsoever for dealing with the onslaught of suffering in our lives. Rather than trying to lock suffering out, we succumb to it and are easily over-whelmed by it. We react by not reacting, except in the most basic and passive of senses. In doing so, we fail to look beyond our suffering. We become blinded by our pain and can no longer see the road before us. At times, we are even driven to extremes. Because we fail to see any meaning in our suffering, we somehow conclude that there is no meaning in life itself.

THE STOICS ~ Still others of us stiffen our upper lips and try to bear our suffering as best we can. We accept its presence in our lives, but convince ourselves that the best way of dealing with it is to be indifferent toward it. This stoical attitude helps us to survive, but at the cost of putting us out of touch with our feelings. We become cold in our relationships with others and the things around us. Detachment becomes our way of operating in the world and of dealing with all that we encounter. We distance ourselves from our suffering and, in doing so, overcome it only to the extent that we distance ourselves from our own humanity.

THE SELF-BLAMERS ~ Others of us blame ourselves for our suffering. We accept what comes to us ungrudgingly because we think we deserve it. Our reasons for thinking this way may vary: a poor self-image, an exaggerated notion of sin, an abusive family history, latent masochistic tendencies, a false image of a vengeful, wrathful God—or any combination of these. More often than not, reacting to suffering in this way is a subtle method of control. Granted that there are times when the suffering that comes our way is genuinely deserved (for example, a just punishment for a crime), to consistently blame ourselves for *every* misfortune we encounter is rooted in the illusory truth that we stand at the center of the universe and that the meaning of suffering is somehow locked up deep within ourselves.

THE PROJECTORS ~ Others of us blame others for our suffering: usually other people (for example, our parents, our teachers, our friends, society, and so on) or God. We do so normally out of a need to locate the origin of our pain. The trouble is we often jump to conclusions by projecting onto others false purposes and ulterior motives that have no basis in reality. Even when others genuinely are the cause of our pain, it is so easy for us to demonize them and make them the external expression of our own sinful inadequacies. Doing this to other people kindles the fires of familial, ethnic, national, and religious hatred; to God, false images of him and the embers of unbelief.

SUFFERING AS HUMAN ~ Finally, others of us look upon suffering not as a part of the problem of our human situation but as part of the solution. Better yet, we tend not to look upon the situation as a problem at all that needs to be solved, but as a mystery that needs to be experienced, journeyed with, and befriended. Here, suffering is embraced as part of the mystery of life that is death, and of death that is life. This view sees suffering as an intrinsic part of the human journey.

Suffering not only teaches us and molds us; it also unites us to each other, by virtue of our common humanity, and to God, by virtue of Christ's suffering and death. The meaning of suffering is a religious question. For Christians, it goes to the heart of the Christ event.

At one time or another in our lives, each of us has probably reacted to suffering in each of these ways. We grow as we journey through life—and often lose our way. It is important for us to be honest about our attitudes toward suffering. There is no sense fooling ourselves by pretending to be more mature or knowledgeable than we really are. The more we understand the reasons why we react the way we do, the better will we be able to understand the meaning of suffering in our lives. Doing so will give us a deeper insight into ourselves and the reasons why the particular suffering we face has crossed our paths.

It will also loosen our load and help us to embrace them with sincere and open hearts.

EMBRACED BY CHRIST

Just what does it mean, though, to embrace the suffering that befalls us? Just how do we go about befriending the pain and turmoil that enters our lives and that we try so hard to avoid? How do we journey with the very thing we have sought for so long to escape? As Christians, embracing suffering means first that we ourselves have been embraced by Christ. Without this fundamental assurance that God has entered our world and, through his own passion and death, embraced our human world, we will never get past square one.

To understand what it means to be embraced by Christ, we have to look at his suffering and death on the cross and ask some very concrete questions about its meaning for our lives. Why, for example, did he have to die on the cross? Could not God have devised some other, less painful way to redeem fallen humanity? Why did God have to assume our human nature? Why was the death of Jesus the God-man so necessary to God's redemptive plan?

Down through the centuries, theologians have given a variety of answers to these probing questions about the suffering of God. For a Church Father like Gregory the Great (d. 604), Jesus' death on the cross involved a grand strategy by which God ransomed humanity back from the snares of Satan. For a medieval monastic writer like Anselm of Canterbury (d. 1109), it was the way in which God's mercy satisfied the demands of God's justice due to the sin of Adam. For a scholastic thinker like Peter Abelard (d. 1142), it was God's way of teaching us how to love. Ransom, satisfaction, moral example: three very different understandings of the cross.

This discussion is not the place to go into great detail about the benefits of these or any other theories of Jesus' suffering and death. For the moment, it suffices to remark that each of these explanations have their merits and their shortcomings. Indeed, no single explanation will ever fully exhaust the mystery of Christ's passion and death. Each provides a glimpse into the meaning of Christ's suffering, but also hides as much as its reveals. The mystery of Christ's passion and death may very well include some facet of each of these explanations—but also so very much more.

The real reason for Jesus' suffering on the cross lies hidden in the mind of God. "For my thoughts are not your thoughts, nor are your ways my ways, says the LORD" (Isa 55:8). The truth is we will probably never understand all the reasons for God acting the way he did in the person of Jesus the Christ. But perhaps we are not meant to understand completely. Perhaps we do not even *need* a detailed explanation. Perhaps it is good enough simply to know that God loves us. Love, after all, imparts a knowledge all its own, the kind which, in the long run, is really all that matters. "God is love," the Scriptures tell us (1 Jn 4:8). The knowledge that this love extends to us is all we need.

THE COMPASSION OF GOD

For today's believers, Jesus' suffering and death is probably best understood as an expression of the compassion of God. The meaning of the word "compassion" is "to suffer with," from the Latin *cum pati*. This theory holds that Jesus died on the cross not to ransom us from Satan, or to satisfy the demands of God's justice, or even merely to teach us the meaning of love, but to join us in our suffering, that is, to *be* with us as we suffer. This understanding of Jesus' passion and death, while not incompatible with the others, goes one step further by stating that Jesus is present to us in a special way in the hardship and suffering that comes to us during our sojourn through life. The suffering and death of Jesus, in other words, is not some historical event that ended when he gave up his spirit on Good Friday, but an event of transhistorical significance which continues down to the present.

This continuation means that, through the passion and death of Christ, human suffering has become a vehicle of encounter with God. Jesus embraced human suffering so that we, in our own suffering, would never be alone in our time of need. Whenever we suffer, whatever kind of suffering it is, Jesus is always there. He who has plumbed the depths of human suffering comes to us in the midst of our afflictions. He embraces our cross with us, whether we want him there or not. He has come to lighten the burden of suffering in our lives. The pain will still be there, no doubt, but he has made himself our companion, a fellow traveler who walks with us every step of the way, even into the shadow of death—and beyond. Never again will we be alone.

This understanding of Jesus' passion and death helps us to see his beatitudes (Mt 5:3–10; Lk 6:20–23) in a new and different light. He blesses the poor, the hungry, the mourners, indeed, all those who suffer, because in his suffering and death they are now united to him in a deep and intimate way. The poor of the world have God's special favor precisely because they are the ones who suffer the most. By his suffering and death, Jesus unites himself with all of suffering humanity, especially that of the outcasts, the poor, and the oppressed: "Truly I tell you, just as you did not do it to one of the least of these, you did not do it to me" (Mt 25:45). Writhing in pain as he hangs from his cross, he blesses an outcast of society, saying: "Today you will be with me in Paradise" (Lk 23:43).

EMBRACING OTHERS

Christ's embrace of our suffering gives us the assurance of God's love for us. It enables us to own our suffering and to find in it an invitation to share more deeply in an intimate relationship with God. That invitation extends not only to us, but to everyone we meet. It bids us to embrace the suffering of others and to recognize our own suffering in theirs.

We can embrace the suffering of others only when we are firmly convinced that Christ has already embraced our own and that the suffering of all humanity is somehow incorporated into the drama of his divine *passio*. That conviction is itself a gift from God—a conviction that enables us to trust God with more and more of our lives. By letting go of our hold over our own suffering—by offering it to Christ—we find ourselves more and more able to allow God's Spirit to work in and through us. "[I]t is no longer I who live, but it is Christ who lives in me" (Gal 2:20). "If we live by the Spirit, let us also be guided by the Spirit" (Gal 5:25). The words of the apostle remind us of the intimate relationship with God we share in Christ. By allowing Christ to live in us, we follow the Spirit's lead and embrace the suffering of those around us.

What does this mean concretely? In the first place, we embrace the suffering of others by entering their world and trying to understand as best we can the full dimensions of their suffering. This entrance into the suffering of others means taking the time to look around, stepping out of our own concerns, and trying to view the world from their point of view. Once we understand something of the nature of their suffering, it then means taking time out of our lives to be with them in their suffering.

Compassion for others requires a sacrifice of time on our part. We cannot show compassion toward those who suffer if we are never with them or if we give them only that part of our lives that fits neatly into our schedule. Showing compassion toward them means living with them, eating and drinking with them, crying with them, laughing with them, grieving with them, mourning with them. More than anything else, it means being with them in their suffering.

Our presence to those who suffer means more to them

33

than one might imagine. Our presence to them is God's presence to us and ultimately manifests itself in the gift of ourselves to them. This gift means doing what we can to alleviate the suffering of those we are with for as long as possible. Just what that is will vary according to the needs of those we are serving and the resources at our disposal. In some cases, we may be able to do a great deal in lessening the suffering of those we are with. At other times, the only thing we may be able to do is be with them in their suffering, pray with them, and assure them that God is closer to them than they think. Presence to those who suffer gives nourishment to their spirits and transforms their pain into meaningful hope.

If all of this seems a bit overwhelming, let us remember that, as individuals, we cannot be present to everyone's suffering, but that as members of Christ's Body the small part we play in our particular time, place, and circumstances, extends with Christ to all the world. Our membership in a community of believers enables us to do more with our meager resources than we could ever do alone. Together, we are able to pool our efforts and put a face on the suffering around us. Together we can encounter the suffering in our midst, befriend it, and find the countenance of our Lord himself in the faces of the poor we serve.

When we truly embrace the suffering of others, we find that it is Christ, all along, who has been embracing them, us, and every other person in the world who has experienced the wrenching pain and heartache of life. Christ's suffering continues down to the present day in the suffering of his Body. That body, his Mystical Body, includes all those living and dead who consciously believe in him plus countless other people of good will who perhaps have never heard of him, but who seek the truth and who try their best to live by that truth. "I am the way, and the truth, and the life" (Jn 14:6). All who suffer, especially the poor, are embraced by Christ and carried with him on his journey through death to new life.

CONCLUSION

We do not know the cause of suffering in the world. Its roots are intimately tied to the problem of evil, a question that has intrigued humanity throughout its collective memory. All we know is that it has made its home in our world and that it continues to wreak havoc in our lives on the physical, psychological, spiritual, and social levels.

Our faith tells us that suffering is not an end in itself and that, because of Christ's death on the cross, it is now common not only to human experience, but also to the divine. Our faith also tells us that God uses all things for the good (Rom 8:28) and that our suffering will not last forever.

Whatever its cause or source of origin, God uses suffering to draw others close. God does so not from a distance, however, but from within. Through the person of Christ, the divinity entered into the depths of human suffering and was able to gather the suffering of *all* of humanity into itself (Jn 12:32). This divine gleaning took place in a concrete historical event which, through the grace of God, has been granted a universal, transhistorical status. The suffering of Christ thus continues down to the present in the suffering of his members, those who make up the vast array of cells, bones, muscles, and sinews that form his Mystical Body, the Church.

The community of the Church embraces the suffering of the world and finds in its face the suffering of Christ who is its head. By being present to those who suffer, the Church is present to Christ, and Christ is present to it. By alleviating the pain of those who suffer, the Church gives witness to that glorious transformation of human suffering that was effected in Christ on Easter morning and which also continues down to the present.

Christ and his Body live for the transformation of human suffering. That transformation comes from God, but is made manifest through the love that God's Spirit pours into the hearts of those who accept the embrace of Christ in their lives and, through it, seek to embrace the suffering of others. That embrace takes on very concrete dimensions in the lives of believers. It propels them to care for the needs of the poor, the oppressed, strangers and prisoners, widows and orphans— all who suffer. That embrace also effects a transformation in them since the more they embrace the suffering of others, the more they experience the embrace of Christ in their own lives.

This explanation is not some starry-eyed fable. The suffering of Christ is as concrete and as relevant today as it was to the earliest believers some two thousand years ago. It gives meaning to our suffering, shows us how to react to our own suffering as well as that of others, and offers us hope in its final transformation. It draws us into the divine embrace and reminds us of our common membership in Christ's Body, which holds out for us the truth of God's ongoing love and concern for our lives. It helps us to view our common humanity in a different light and enables us to accept all things, even the sufferings which come our way, as gifts to be accepted with sincere and humble thanks.

SURVEYING YOUR SKILLS

1. What is your suffering like? Is it primarily physical? Mental? Emotional? Spiritual? Social? What combination of these dimensions of human suffering would best describe your experience?

2. How do you react to suffering? Are you paralyzed by it? Are you overwhelmed by it? Do you try to be indifferent to it? Do you blame yourself for it? Do you blame others for it? Do you blame God for it? Do you accept it? Befriend it? Try to learn from it? Which combination of these possible reactions best describes your relationship to the suffering in your life?

3. Do you consider your suffering to be more or less the same as anyone else's? Is suffering nothing more than a part of being human? What is unique about your suffering? How has it shaped your understanding of yourself? Of others? Of God?

4. What was Jesus' own suffering like? Which dimensions of human suffering did it embrace? How did he react to his suffering? Why did he suffer so? Could his suffering have been avoided? Does his suffering have anything to do with your own? If so, how?

5. Do you bring your suffering to God? Do you share it with God? With Jesus? With the Holy Spirit? Do you ask God to relieve it? To heal you? To show you the meaning of your suffering? What is the relationship between your suffering and your prayer? Do you pray more when you suffer? Less? About the same? Do you remember your suffering? Ignore it? Try to forget it?

4
HEALING OUR MEMORIES
~
THE FOURTH STEP

Therefore, I will pass beyond even memory, so that I may attain to him who has set me apart from four-footed animals and made me wiser than the birds of the air. Even beyond memory will I pass, so that I may find you—where? O truly good and certain delight, so that I may find you where? If I find you apart from memory, I am unmindful of you. How then shall I find you, if I do not remember you?

Augustine, *The Confessions*, X.17[6]

Children learn to walk through trial and error. This method means that they must remember past mistakes, look beyond them, and seek new ways for reaching their goals. If they could not remember their mistakes, they would be doomed to make them over and over again. That is precisely what happens to us when learning to walk by faith. If we don't remember our mistakes and learn from them, we will most likely repeat them.

Where would we be without memory? We would not know who we were—as individuals or as a people. We would not be aware of what happened to us the day before, let alone the months or years previous to it. We would have no awareness of time, no history, no sense of self. We would go through the day without being aware of what we have done. We would not look to the future, for it would be indistinguishable from the present or the past. Only a person with a sense of the past can appreciate the present. Only a person of memory can understand what it means to relish a moment, let it go, retrieve it, and relish it again. Only a person of memory can wait in joyful expectation of what is still to come.

A DEEPER DIMENSION

Remembering calls forth another dimension of life, one that cannot be seen when something is first experienced. When we remember, we place an event in perspective. We see it in relation to other occurrences in our lives. We interpret it and find meaning in it. Remembering enables us not to live in the past, but to use it in such a way so as to understand our present. When we recall a particular event in our lives, we are able to appreciate it in a way we could not at the moment it happened.

Remembering sheds light on a dimension of life that only the passage of time can reveal. When we look back on our lives and recall particular events and happenings, we go through a process of selection. It would be next to impossible to remember *every* impression, *every* experience (good or bad), *every* event that happens to us. What we are able to remember has touched us and tells us something about who we are and the type of persons we have become.

Our memories accompany us through life. They are our lifelong companions—for good or for ill. We can learn from them or be blinded by them, allow them to teach us or shroud us in ignorance, use them to make or to evade decisions. Our past helps to shape our present. Our memory of it can free us or enslave us; liberate us or ruin us.

The Jews have been described as a people looking backward while walking into the future, that is, as a people who carry their past around with them wherever they go. This attitude toward life and their history has molded them into a people with a strong sense of tradition and religious identity. Their memory of their past affirms them and propels them into the future. As they look back, they remember both good times and bad: times of liberation and wandering, of conquest and defeat, of exile and return.

Through it all, they became a people with a deep sense of God's continual involvement in their lives. They may have abandoned God at one time or another, but God never abandoned them. God promised to be faithful to them to the end of time. For this reason, Jews have always been a people of great hope.

We, too, must look backward while walking into the future. If we do not carry our past with us, we will become individuals without a past, a people without a history. We carry our past with us by remembering it, by reflecting upon it, by learning from it, by celebrating it. In doing so, we encounter ourselves in ways we never before thought possible. We get new insights into why we act the way we do, about the kind of people we have become, about who we are and what it is we hope to become.

In looking back on the past, we eventually receive an entirely different way of looking at time. It becomes not our adversary, with whom we are constantly vying, but a friend who walks beside us in our sojourn through life. This new attitude toward time helps us to embrace everything in our past and accept it as part of who we are and who we are striving to become.

Once we embrace our past in this manner, the process of healing can begin. Memories which, perhaps for years, have weighed us down and prevented us from maturing as individuals, rise to the surface of our minds, are dealt with judiciously, and gently released. When we befriend our past rather than ignore it or run away from it, we grow in wisdom and deepen our relationship with God.

REMEMBERED BY GOD

"Can a woman forget her nursing child, or show no compassion for the child of her womb? Even these may forget, yet I will not forget you" (Isa 49:15). God may be irrelevant to us, but we are always relevant to God. Of all the things we forget in life, probably the most important is that we are children of a loving and caring God.

It may sound strange for us to think of God as someone who remembers us. We like to think of God as being too busy to be concerned about the likes of us. Out of the billions of galaxies, the countless stars, and innumerable planets in the heavens, one would think that God would have better things to do than to look out for our individual welfare. But God *does* care. The Divine Self showers existence on us at every moment. We are alive and breathing, we can see and smell, hear, feel and taste, we can think, speak, and act freely only because God remembers us and preserves us in life.

How does God remember and preserve us? What precisely do we mean when we speak of God's memory? God, who gives expression to the Word, recollects that Word eternally. This recollection is distinct from God, yet also *is* God. The memory of that Word is different from the power of thought that generates it. Thought, Word, Memory: Father, Son, Spirit. The memory of God is intimately tied up in the divine relations of the Trinity. It is the eternal interaction between the generating thought of God and the Word it produces. This interaction reveals the depths of the divine being and is known to us as Spirit.

God's memory, however, is more than an eternal recollection of the Divine Self. In the person of Jesus, it has entered our world in a new and definitive way. This embrace by Jesus of our human situation offers us the possibility that our own powers of recollection might one day participate in the divine. In every eucharistic celebration, Christ remembers in his Body and his Body in him. Together in the Spirit, we offer eternal praise to the Father and, in so doing, share more deeply in the intimate relationships of the Trinity.

In the Eucharist, we remember Christ's offering and are remembered through Christ in the Spirit by the Father. The New Covenant is thus made present in every act of liturgical worship. In Christ, all of who we are—our past, present, and future—is offered to the Father in a single, all-encompassing action of love.

Christ's love for us never fades. It is that love which works in our hearts and heals the wounds of our souls. Once healed, our wounded memories free us to be the people we are called to be for ourselves and for those around us.

UNCOVERING OUR MEMORIES

Our memories, however, are often not so easily healed. Many of us have been hurt by life. Some of us have been so deeply wounded that our memories of what happened to us have been repressed and deeply embedded in our unconscious. We do not remember what happened, but we bear the terrible consequences in our present lives of those long-ago hurts. As a result, some of us are sad, depressed, and angry people who often inflict our unhappiness on others even when we do not intend to. Thus, people keep their distance from us. They are careful about what they say and are always on their guard when they are around us. In such instances, our buried memories haunt us in both our sleeping and waking hours and prevent us from becoming the people we are meant to be.

SURFACING THE EMBEDDED WOUNDS ~ How do we deal with wounds that have embedded themselves so deeply in our psyches? In the first place, we need to bring them to the surface. This uncovering in itself is sometimes a long and painful process, one where another's help may be needed. We begin the uncovering process by making a thorough inventory of our behaviors, focusing especially on those patterns of actions which cause us unhappiness or even just embarrassment, and which we would like to change. We should be as honest with ourselves as possible and try to see ourselves the way others see us. Why do we act this particular way toward this particular person or type of person? What is it that sets us off? Why is it that we are angry or moody, abnormally silent or combative when we come into contact with a certain person, or when we find ourselves in a particular social setting or even when we are alone? The more we are able to identify unhealthy patterns of behavior in our lives, the better.

We should take our time in allowing this process of identification to take place. Deeply rooted habits of behavior usually take a long time to develop and often require a long time to identify. We need to be patient with ourselves when trying to unravel the complexities of our actions.

IDENTIFYING THE EMOTIONS BEHIND THE WOUNDS
~ Once we have identified those unhealthy patterns of behavior that we would like to change in our lives, we need to dig beneath them and try to identify as much as possible the emotions behind them. We are not disembodied spirits who act apart from our feelings. If we are honest with ourselves, we will find that our actions are closely associated with the way we feel.

In healthy patterns of behavior, a certain harmony exists between our actions and our emotions. This harmony exists because we have taken the time to listen to our feelings, befriend them, and allow them to participate in our conscious lives. In unhealthy patterns of behavior, we have not allowed this process to take place. As a result, we ignore the emotional side of our lives and usually wind up acting them out in destructive ways.

Someone once said that we are depressed because we are angry, that we are angry because we are hurt, and that we are hurt because we did not get what we need. The more we are able to identify the feelings behind our unhealthy patterns of behavior (indeed, even the feelings behind the feelings), the easier it will be for us to befriend them and integrate them into our lives.

INVENTORY OF PAINFUL MEMORIES ~ It is not enough, however, simply to identify the feelings behind our unhealthy habits of action. Behind the feelings there are memories and experiences that may have happened long ago, or very recently. These memories can be relatively easy to recall—or difficult. They can be central to our awareness and drift through our minds many times each day, or they can exist only on the periphery of our conscious lives and require great effort on our part to bring them to the fore. We can also be completely unaware of them and need to give them time to rise to the surface of our conscious awareness.

At this stage, we need to make a thorough inventory of all the painful experiences that have made us feel the way we do. Recognizing them is the first step to understanding them. And while understanding them does not guarantee that we will be able to change them, it does make us more aware of what needs to be done, and the distance we still must travel along the road to wholeness.

PLUMBING THE UNCONSCIOUS ~ Finally, we must deal with the repressed memories, those painful experiences that have passed from our consciousness into the realm of the unconscious. Even though these buried memories are the most difficult to identify, largely because they have passed out of our conscious control, they are often the memories that are most closely connected to our unhealthy patterns of behavior. To get in touch with them, we need to pay more attention to the way in which the unconscious impinges on our daily experience.

Dreams, in particular, are one way in which our unconscious speaks to us and brings to the surface particular images, symbols, and memories that have particular relevance to our daily lives. The meaning of a dream depends on the dreamer. Only he or she can unlock the mystery that it is trying to communicate. Very often, it helps to write dreams down, especially the recurrent ones, in order to see if any recognizable pattern emerges. By reflecting on them and by sitting with them, we often gain much insight into the meaning of our conscious activity.

The relationship between our behaviors, feelings, thoughts, and unconscious memories is cyclical rather than linear. This means that the two ends of the spectrum—that is, behaviors and unconscious memories—eventually connect. If we do not go through the process of identifying our behaviors and then understanding the feelings, thoughts, and repressed memories behind them, then it is highly likely that we will act out of the unknown forces deep in our unconscious. When this occurs, we do not understand why we act the way we do. This lack of integration and self-understanding is a major obstacle to our conversion and the healing of memories for which we long.

HEALING OUR MEMORIES

We can enter into and try to understand the ongoing cycle of behaviors, feelings, thoughts, and unconscious memories in our lives at any stage. What is important is not where we begin, but that we enter into the cycle and try to uncover the reasons behind our actions. In doing so, we will discover something more of who we are. That discovery is facilitated because being and doing are so intimately related in our lives. Who we are is intricately related to what we do—and vice versa. The more we understand the one, the better will we be able to deal with the other.

Self-understanding, however, is still not enough. We may understand ourselves very well—perhaps all too well—yet still not be able to change. The fact that we have allowed our hurts and deeply repressed memories to rise to the surface of our awareness does not necessarily mean that they will be resolved. For healing to take place in our lives, we need not only to recognize our limitations and weaknesses, but also admit that we are incapable of changing ourselves. We need to turn to others for help, and in a special way to God.

Only God can heal our deepest hurts, our sins, our failings. For a true healing of memories to take place we need to recognize the place of God in our lives, bare open our hearts, and allow the Holy Spirit to work in us. For this to happen, we must be humble enough to admit our inability to change what needs to be changed in our lives; we must also be willing to trust God and risk everything.

We do this through a simple prayer of remembering, during which, using our imagination, we carefully go back over every stage of our lives—the time in our mother's womb, our infancy and childhood, our adolescence and young adulthood, our growth to maturity, our middle age, our older years and the approach of death—allowing the particular hurts to surface and placing all that we remember (and do not remember) before the Lord. At each stage of this great act of remembering, we ask God to heal us: "Heal me, Lord, heal me! Have mercy on me, and heal me." When prayed with sincerity and with complete honesty, this simple prayer from the heart will reap a harvest of plenty.

The prayer of remembering helps us to recall those painful moments in our lives, but also invites God into our lives as an active force in our ongoing conversion. We invite God to be with us as we go back into our lives. We ask God to forgive those who have done us any harm and ask for the grace to let go of any pain and bitterness that we still may be harboring deep within us. We ask God to cast out all the fears in our lives and ask in a special way that we be forgiven the many times that we have acted out of these fears rather than out of the love of others. In time, this simple prayer of remembering enables us to let go of the hurts which have for so long disfigured our souls.

In time, God's healing hand will dig down deep within us and remove the ugly scars that years of repression and neglect have inflicted on our hearts. In time, we will put up no defenses against the Spirit of God as we give it room to spread its wings within our souls and fly on the shifting currents of our vast interior spaces. In time, we ourselves will begin to follow the Spirit's lead and find ourselves moving in concert with its spontaneous internal promptings.

God promises not only to heal our memories, but to elevate our hearts and enable them to share in the great divine remembering of the Father's love for the Son and the Son's love for the Father that is Spirit. This remembering is going on even now as you read this book. It promises to change our lives, both now and forever. Once we partake of it, our lives will never be the same.

CONCLUSION

We are creatures of habit, habits deeply ingrained in our memories. We cannot function without memory. We fear many things in life, but very few fears inspire as great a sense of dread as that of losing our memory. Losing it would be for us a living death. We would no longer recognize those closest to us. Our family and friends would be strangers to us. We would be a people without a home, without a country, without a heritage, without beliefs. We would not know what little we *do* know of God.

Life would be a pale reflection of our present experience. We would be awake, but not aware; we would see, but not understand; we would live, but not recall. It is hard for us to imagine what life would be like without memory. That we can appreciate it and mourn its possible loss reveals its importance to us. Without memory, our minds would be blind to the passage of time; thought would not be what we now know it to be. We would be impoverished and not even know it.

Memory is one of God's most precious gifts to us. Without it, we would be set adrift in a vast sea of experiences with no means of orienting ourselves aright. Memories enable us to touch and to taste the deeper dimensions of life. Through them, we delve beneath the appearances and are able to sense the particular meaning in the events and the encounters that fill our lives. When we remember, we bring the past to the present and make it a part of our future. The more we do this, the wiser we become; the easier it is for us to uncover those areas of hurt in our lives that prevent us from being the people God calls us to be.

God remembers us and promises to heal us. For this to happen, however, we must identify the unhealthy patterns of behavior in our lives and get in touch with the feelings and memories—both conscious and unconscious—that perpetuate them. Naming them, however, is not quite enough. We must also turn to God and humbly ask for a healing of these hurtful memories. The prayer of remembering is that process whereby we open up these hurts and ask God to heal them and transform them. Through this prayer—itself a precious gift from God—we allow God's Spirit to move within us and enable us to share more deeply in the inner life of God.

We are a people of memory, because God is a God of memory. Created in the divine image and likeness, we come to a deeper knowledge of ourselves through our ability to reflect on our lives, remember all that has happened to us, and integrate those experiences into our own self-understanding.

What happens to us in time is but a faint reflection of the ever-deepening process of remembering that occurs in God for all eternity. As we enter more deeply into the divine life, we share more deeply in the divine remembering, a process which includes God's own remembering of ourselves. As we grow in the knowledge of the Lord, we thus grow in knowledge of ourselves. God, who has blessed us with the precious gift of memory, eventually allows us, in time, to see ourselves as we are seen by Christ. When this occurs, God's active remembering overshadows whatever is lacking in our own memories. Then our own memories will have finally been healed and transformed by grace to reflect for all time the grandeur and the glory of God.

SURVEYING YOUR SKILLS

1. What role does remembering play in your daily existence? Can you picture yourself functioning in life without a memory? What would it be like to lack this ability? Do you consider memory a blessing or a curse? Does it help you get through the day or does it make you a prisoner of the past?

2. What pleasant memories come to mind when you look back to your childhood? To your adolescent years? To your young adulthood? To your middle age? To your older years? What painful memories come to mind for these same periods of your life? Do you look back on your life with gratitude or with sadness? With happiness or regret?

3. Are you conscious of any memories in your life that are in need of healing? How long have you been aware of them? How do they make you feel? How do they affect your image of yourself? How do they affect the way you act with others? With God?

4. Do you believe that you are remembered by God? Do you believe that God cares for you as an individual? Do you believe this in your heart? Do you think there is anything in your life that God is not concerned about? Do you believe in your heart that God will never forget you?

5. Do you ever ask God to heal you of those memories that weigh you down and inhibit you from leading a healthy life? Do you believe that God has the power to heal you in these areas? Do you believe this in your heart?

5
CHANGING OUR HEARTS

THE FIFTH STEP

> A pure heart is perhaps one which has no natural
> propulsion towards anything in any manner what-
> soever. When in its extreme simplicity such a heart
> has become like a writing-tablet beautifully
> smoothed and polished, God comes to dwell in it
> and writes there His own laws.
>
> Maximos the Confessor,
> *Two Hundred Texts on Theology: Second Century*, 81[7]

Children learn by imitating others. As they do so,
their image of themselves begins to change, for they
now are not only capable of distinguishing themselves
from their surroundings but also actively interact with them
in a way that they could never do before. That change in self-
image is but one of a series of changes that will occur to them
throughout the rest of their childhood and, indeed, throughout the rest of their lives.

Our walk in faith follows a similar course. We, too, learn by
imitation: our parents, our teachers, our friends and, most of all,
Jesus. For this role modeling to occur, we must undergo a series
of internal shifts in the way we view and understand ourselves.

This shift means putting aside our stubbornness and letting go of our carefully laid out plans. It means entertaining
the possibility that we may not have all the answers, that some-

thing more is required of us. It means changing our hearts: integrating our feelings, opening our minds, listening to the Spirit. It means looking at the world with different eyes and seeing what before we all too easily overlooked.

BREAKING UP THE STONE

"I will remove the heart of stone from their flesh and give them a heart of flesh" (Ezek 11:19). Conversion begins not with us, but with God. Something happens and we are never again the same. Sometimes conversion is dramatic, but more often than not it involves a subtle and gradual change in our lives. God touches our hearts and moves us to do things we never before contemplated. Our coldness and indifference toward others begins to fade. We feel weak and humbled. We no longer feel in control of our lives. We no longer see ourselves at the center of things.

Conversion encompasses every aspect of our lives. It is more than just intellectual assent to the truths of the faith. It means loving God and neighbor with all our heart, mind, soul, and strength (Lk 10:27). We need conversion because we are always holding something back, because there will always be more room in our hearts for love. We trust God with our lives, but not quite enough. We see Christ in our neighbors, but not quite enough. We follow the promptings of the Spirit in our lives, but not quite completely. Everything we attempt falls somewhat short of the mark. God wants *all* of our love, *all* of our affections, *all* of our desire. God wants us to be full of the divine life.

Conversion is that process which frees us from self-interest and fills us with the love of God. Such a process normally goes on in us for a lifetime. At every moment of every day of our lives, the call to conversion sounds in our hearts. We may not hear it. There may be too much noise and clutter in our lives for that. But the call sounds nonetheless.

Conversion sounds in our hearts—and waits. It looks for the right moment, for just the right place, just the right circumstance. It swells in our unconscious and rises up in our dreams and fantasies. It makes us restless. We feel too comfortable with our present situation. Something needs changing.

We first look to externals, but see that they get us nowhere. We are not satisfied with living on the surface of life, on the level of appearances. We want to live life at its depth and so turn to the heart. It is there where the work must be done, there where it all begins. God wants our hearts, not our sacrifices; our undivided love, not piecemeal promises. God wants to be God in our lives, not a part-time interest or secondary concern. It is God who removes our stony hearts, not ourselves. In some cases, such as Paul's conversion on the road to Damascus (Acts 9:1–9), this change takes place in an instant. In most cases, however, it is a long, drawn-out process. Deep-seated prejudices must be cracked open and chipped away; selfish attitudes, unearthed and hauled off; bad habits, rooted out and destroyed. Our stony hearts must be broken up and carted away piece by piece.

God will not remove what we refuse to part with. The more we cling, the longer the process of removal will take. For most of us, conversion of life is a long and painful experience. It means letting go of some of the things most precious to us and allowing God to rearrange many of our most closely held beliefs.

A heart of stone is no heart at all. It cannot replenish the body with the precious fluids of life. A heart of stone symbolizes heaviness, stagnation, and death. We who have one know nothing of mercy and compassion. We turn our backs on those in need. We ignore the weak and the helpless. We have no time for those less fortunate than ourselves. We know nothing of life. We walk among the dead. Nothing can take root and grow in our hearts. We are as lifeless as statues, as cold and foreboding as the stones which will one day mark our graves.

How we got in such a state is not easy to explain. Something in us turns from God and prefers to wander. We want to go our own way in life. We set out on our own and soon forget the reason why we were put here. We are guided by our own selfish desires for pleasure, wealth, and power. These desires become the commandments that govern our lives, the rules by which we live. We seek only what will benefit us, only what we can gain for ourselves. We are willing to use other people, to walk over them if necessary in order to get what we want. We show little or no remorse for what we have done. We convince ourselves that we are in the right. We are not even conscious of what we are becoming.

Despite our unacceptable actions, however, God refuses to give up on us. The Spirit blows where it wills. It weathers the stone within us and wears it down; waters of life seep down into the cracks and swell them open. Gradually over time, a measurable change takes place: the stone has broken up and turned to gravel; the gravel then turns to granules of sand. What once kept us from life now seeps out of our hearts like the sands of an hourglass. In God's own time, our stony hearts are broken up and carried away. The only obstacle is our own stubbornness and refusal to change.

CONVERTING THE HEART

When we undergo a process of conversion, we become men and women of compassion. We are able to feel deeply for the poor and brokenhearted. We see ourselves in their place. We understand that, before God, all are impoverished.

During this conversion process, God gives us back our human hearts. We recognize that we are made of flesh and blood. We come to accept our human limitations—in ourselves and in others. We accept ourselves as we are and recognize that our journey to God is accomplished primarily by God and that the most we can do is get out of the way. Even getting out of the way cannot be done without God's help.

God gives us back our capacity for human feeling. This gift—itself a work of his Spirit—initiates an even longer process of divinization in our lives. "God became human so that we might become divine."[8] This well-known soteriological principle is also the fundamental principle of conversion in our lives. God removes our stony hearts and gives us back our natural hearts; God then takes our natural hearts and divinizes them, conforming them unto his own.

Our hearts remain flesh and blood, but are elevated, given the capacity to love in a way that they were never capable of before. All of this is possible because of Jesus. His heart is human, but also divine. When we partake of his life, we are immersed in his heart. We become like him in all things, just as he became like us in every way (Heb 2:17).

The conversion wrought in us by God enables us to live a life of the Spirit. We become sensitive to its movement in our lives. We are able to peer through the various rationalizations we use to explain our indifference and inactivity before the face of poverty and injustice. We are moved to respond to the real needs of the people with whom we come into contact. We open our hearts and welcome those in need. We try to find a way to reach out to them and lighten their load. Our lives become a continuous effort to live for others. In so doing, we become men and women who live for God.

THE LEVELS OF CONVERSION

Conversion in our lives goes on at many levels: the personal, the communal, and the societal. Although all of these levels share a reciprocal relationship, the personal dimension is the most fundamental. If we do not undergo a fundamental change of heart and open ourselves to a personal relationship with

Jesus, there is little hope for the transformation of the community to which we belong or for our society as a whole. That is not to say that communal and societal structures do not have a strong influence on our personal lives. This statement only recognizes that their influence wanes before the personal influence of a loving God in the deepest recesses of the human heart.

PERSONAL CONVERSION ~ What precisely do we mean by personal conversion? To begin with, it entails *metanoia* or change of heart, that is, turning our lives around in such a way that God becomes the central focus of everything we do. Personal conversion embraces every dimension of who we are: the physical, psychological, intellectual, spiritual, and social. It occurs slightly differently in each of us depending, to a great degree, on our own personal makeup.

For some, personal conversion occurs first in the mind and then makes its way into the other dimensions of their being. For others, it is primarily a spiritual experience; for still others, it involves a change in lifestyle, an emotional experience, or taking a look at their ways of relating to others. However it begins, it is not complete until every part of us is permeated with gospel values.

Obviously, this permeation would be difficult for someone who lives in an environment that does not actively support those values, but it is not impossible. Some of the Church's greatest saints made their way to holiness in the face of very trying circumstances, while some of its greatest sinners were given all the advantages conceivable for making their way to God.

COMMUNITY CONVERSION ~ We are social beings by nature. From the moment we are born we exist in a social environment. Much of what we learn about life, about ourselves, about society, about God, we learn in our earliest social environment, that is, in the family. Some community atmospheres are more conducive than others for instilling gospel values. In one way or another, all of them are a little dysfunctional. (Remember, there is only *one* holy family!)

Conversion on this social level means shaping our relationships within the community so that they allow us to deepen our relationship to God. It means looking at the way we relate to one another, identifying what is wrong and how it can be improved. Very often, all it takes is learning how to listen better to one another. Once we take time to listen to one another's stories, especially those closest to us, we find that their story is not really all that different from our own.

Conversion on the communal level also entails looking at the way we, as a community, relate to the larger society and to the world. The community to which we belong buffers us from the world, interprets it for us, and mediates our interaction with it. A community imbued with gospel values will play a constructive role in the personal conversion of its members as well as in the transformation of the larger society.

SOCIETAL CONVERSION ～ We are called to preach the gospel to the ends of the earth (Acts 1:8). The Good News of Jesus Christ seeks to permeate every level of human society: the personal, the communal, even the societal.

On the societal level, conversion means identifying those structures in the national and international arenas that prevent people from living fully human and dignified lives. Societal conversion makes use of peaceful, nonviolent means to change unjust social structures which keep people impoverished and do not give them the chance to better their lives. It seeks to defend the rights of the unborn, the terminally sick, the aged, and the economically poor.

The conversion of society is something all Christians must work for. We realize, however, that this conversion takes place in small steps and, at times, is barely visible to the human eye. The City of God and the City of Man have been struggling against one another for centuries—and will continue to do so until the end of time. Society's final transformation lies beyond our own meager efforts to change it. We are not alone in our efforts, however. Christ, who promises to transform the world and all things in it, lives and moves in us. As members of his Body we believe that he is presently working through us and will eventually draw all of humanity to himself.

"Restore us to yourself, O LORD, that we may be restored" (Lam 5:21). Conversion on each of these levels is primarily a work of God and only secondarily our own. It is also multifaceted, involving many dimensions of human existence. Using the analogy of a human person, we might say that each of these levels includes physical, psychological, intellectual, spiritual, and social aspects. Conversion is not complete until each and every one of these dimensions is permeated by a love of God and neighbor. The complexity of the process should not make us lose heart, but make us turn to God all the more in prayer for the coming of the kingdom.

THE NEED FOR PRAYER

"Pray without ceasing" (1 Thess 5:17). These words of the apostle are intimately tied to the call to conversion. We must pray always because we are in constant need of growth. If we refuse to pray, God will not help us to mature in our faith. Our hearts will remain stony; our relationships, empty; our lives, without love.

The more we pray, the more will the Spirit move within us and transform us. We need not worry about what to say or how to say it: "The Spirit helps us in our weakness; for we do not know how to pray as we ought, but that very Spirit intercedes with sighs too deep for words" (Rom 8:26). God helps us with our prayer. God, in fact, inspires it, and gives us the grace to pour out our hearts. God uses prayer to effect in us a life of constant conversion. It is impossible to pray sincerely and not be drawn closer to God. "Ask, and it will be given you; search, and you will find" (Lk 11:9).

When we pray, we should ask God to change our hearts, to help us turn every aspect of our lives over to the power of the gospel. How we pray and what we pray for is largely determined by our relationship to God. When we ask for the grace of conversion, we are looking to deepen our relationship with God. God hears our prayers and is sure to respond. The answer may not be what we were hoping for. God often asks the unexpected of us; we may or may not be ready to concur.

We need to pray not just for ourselves, but also for others. We need to pray not just for those we know, but for those we don't. We need to pray for entire groups of people: families, parishes, organizations, governments, peoples and nations, the whole human race.

Prayer has the power to effect change in people's lives. We should not underestimate its power: "But for God all things are possible" (Mt 19:26). When we pray for others, we extend our love to them. What greater gift could a person give to another than the opportunity for a deep, intimate relationship with God? That is precisely what we do when we make a sincere prayer from the heart for the conversion of others.

We also need to ask others to join us in prayer. Something happens when we join our voices in heartfelt prayer to the Lord. Our own hearts become lighter, more grateful, more subject to change. We sense the Lord's presence in those with whom we pray.

Prayer is the most important activity of our lives. Without it, we have no hope of seeing God face-to-face. Asking someone to pray for us is not an easy thing to do. It requires humility and trust. It involves a certain element of risk. We need others to pray for us, and they need us to pray for them. God uses prayer to draw us closer to each other.

Prayer is not a particularly difficult activity. It is one of the easiest activities of all. God even helps us. Yet, still, for whatever reason, we find reasons to avoid praying. We cherish our independence and somehow think we will lose it when we turn to God. We have convinced ourselves that prayer is a luxury of life, something we can do without, or turn to only as a last resort. Nothing could be further from the truth. Prayer is the beginning and end of the spiritual life. The injunction to never cease praying holds true not just for our present lives, but for what lies beyond.

Prayer is a fountain of joy and an immeasurable source of love. When we walk the way of prayer, we walk the way of conversion. We cannot have one without the other.

CONCLUSION

Conversion involves a change of heart that pours over into every other element of human existence: the physical, psychological, intellectual, spiritual, and social. It can take place in an instant but, as is more likely the case, conversion is a long, drawn-out process that can last a whole lifetime. Conversion is not our own doing, but a work of God. The most we can do is get out of the way and allow the Spirit to accomplish its work in our lives. Even our prayer is something that is inspired in us by the Spirit.

There is no preset pattern of behavior that will guarantee us conversion. "The wind blows where it chooses" (Jn 3:8)—as does the Spirit. The way the Spirit will work in our lives will vary from individual to individual. Solitude is necessary to hear the voice of God crying in the wilderness within us, but its expression in our lives cannot be reduced to a particular series of meditations or actions that will guarantee insight. We must be ready to rest in the silence of our souls as conversion presents itself to us in our lives. We must be ready to listen to the voice of God and say out loud and without hesitation, "Speak, for your servant is listening" (1 Sam 3:10).

Those of us who refuse to stop and listen to the voice of God within us have no hope of finding our way to God. Our hearts will weigh us down and hold us back. They will be too heavy to carry on the journey ahead.

Conversion is intimately connected to a life of prayer. The deeper our life of prayer, the further along we are on the way of conversion. Without prayer, we cannot grow. Without real and substantial growth in our lives, we cannot find God. We who are in constant need of conversion must pray for the grace to pray continually so that we will be able to discern the movement of the Spirit in our lives and know which way we should walk.

Without prayer we easily lose touch with the gentle breeze of the Spirit blowing within us. Once that happens, we lose our sense of direction and find ourselves wandering in a vast wasteland of uncertain truths and cultural relativities. Whether we will ever find our way out depends on whether we are willing to admit our mistakes and turn to God for help. God never refuses, but always answers our prayers. The response may not be what we expected, but it is what we need at the time.

A life of conversion is a life of prayer is a life of trust. We trust God with our lives, believing that everything that happens to us comes out of his deep concern for our lives. God comes to us and never leaves us. It is we who leave God: not once, but time and time again. Like the prodigal son (Lk 15: 11–32), we leave God and return; leave God and return. The marvel of it all is that God is always ready and willing to take us back.

SURVEYING YOUR SKILLS

1. What kind of heart do you have? A stony one? A natural, fleshy one? Something in-between? What areas of your life need to be broken up, ground down, and carted off?

On the physical level? On the mental and emotional levels? On the spiritual and social levels?

2. Is conversion for you primarily personal, communal, or societal? Does one have a priority over the other? How do these various dimensions relate? How do they manifest themselves concretely in your life?

3. How does conversion come about in your life? Do you view it as something involving your own personal effort? The effort of others? How does God's activity enter into it?

4. What is the relationship between prayer and conversion? Do you pray to God for your own conversion? For the conversion of others? For the conversion of the Church? For the conversion of society? For the conversion of the world?

5. How do you pray for conversion? Be as specific as possible. Does your prayer encompass every dimension of your being? Do you pray to God with your whole heart, mind, soul, and strength? Is your prayer time an essential part of your day? Does it draw you closer to God?

6
FOSTERING INTIMACY

~

THE SIXTH STEP

We tend to identify ourselves with those we love.
We try to enter into their own souls and become
what they are, thinking as they think, feeling as they
feel, and experiencing what they experience. But
there is no true intimacy between souls who do not
know how to respect another's solitude. I cannot
be united in love with a person whose very personality my love tends to obscure, to absorb, and to
destroy. Nor can I awaken true love in a person
who is invited, by my love, to be drowned in the act
of drowning me with love.

Thomas Merton, *No Man Is An Island*[9]

*E*ven before children learn how to walk, they interact with and start to reach out to others. Learning
how to walk enables them to reach out even more.
Their search for playmates and, later on, friends and lifelong
companions will take them down many roads and thorough-
fares. Some of these roads will be dead ends; others will bring
them further along their journey.

Our walk of faith involves a similar search for close, intimate ties. We all long for someone who knows us as we really are, someone who allows us to relax, take our shoes off,
and talk freely about the things we care about. We desire a

friend we can trust, someone who will never let us down, who will be there for us when trouble comes and nothing seems to make sense. We want to be listened to. We wish to be treated with dignity and respect. We yearn to give love and receive it in return.

Although we all long for intimacy, few of us really know what it is. We mistake the externals for the inner essence, its trappings for its substance. Intimacy cannot be planned or programmed. It comes often when it is least expected. It can occur between any two people, even between incompatible types. It involves a close communion of hearts, a knowledge of another that comes by spending time and sharing with that person.

Intimate sharing goes beneath the surface of things. It shuns appearances and seeks to experience life at its depth. On that level, people are able to talk about the things that really matter to them: their hopes and dreams, their anxieties and fears, their losses and regrets. Such sharing creates a bond between persons. When we feel known and appreciated by someone, we experience the world around us differently. We become more open and welcoming in our dealings with others. We appreciate the simplest things in life and wonder how our eyes could have been closed for so long.

Without intimacy, life becomes a drudgery and hardly worth living. Those without intimate relationships lead isolated and lonely lives. They feel hollow inside and spend much of their time trying to fill their emptiness with false and unlikely substitutes. They cannot walk in faith for they have never learned the ways of trust.

CROSSING THE DISTANCE

Even the closest and most intimate of friends were once total strangers. It takes a long time to develop the trust of a deep, lasting friendship. Becoming intimate with another person requires us to traverse the barriers that separate us. It means risking rejection and making ourselves vulnerable to another's judgment. It takes courage to step out of ourselves and to reach out to another. We do not know how the other person will react. Our overtures may not be reciprocated. We may meet with coldness, or indifference, or outright rebuff.

There is no simple formula that will automatically draw two people together. No two people are the same; no two relationships are exactly alike. What draws some together may pull others apart. The secret to intimacy is not to control it, but to allow it to unfold.

Intimacy involves a deeply spiritual encounter between two people. The best way to find it is to encounter our inner selves. It is impossible to share deeply with another person if we ourselves have nothing to share. It is not possible to know another person if we know nothing of ourselves. Knowledge of the self is a basic requirement of all intimate relationships. The more we know about ourselves, the more will we be able to share with others and allow them to do so with us. We know more about ourselves by spending time alone and listening to our hearts. For this to happen, we must relish the moments of solitude that come our way and foster a contemplative spirit in our lives.

"By wisdom is a house built, and by understanding it is established" (Prov 24:3). Intimacy with another requires first that we understand ourselves. We must be willing to cross that distance within us that separates us from ourselves. We must be willing to befriend our deepest, truest selves and allow that self to rise within us and permeate our conscious and unconscious thoughts. Only by communing with ourselves will we learn what it means to commune with another. Only by taking the risk of self-knowledge will we be able to trust ourselves enough to allow another person to come to know us.

KEEPING THE BOUNDARIES

Putting time aside for us to get to know ourselves helps us to recognize its importance to others. We must allow others the space to be themselves and to come to know themselves better. Intimacy thrives on solitude. Solitude, however, is very fragile and can be easily upset, especially in those who are just beginning to walk down the path of self-knowledge. Intimacy requires us to keep firm boundaries in our relationships with others. We must keep a balance, walk the fine line between the extremes of isolation and intrusion. Most of us arrive at this balance through trial and error and by learning from our mistakes.

What kind of boundaries are we talking about? For one thing, we must give the other person the freedom and the space to be alone. Only in solitude can anyone delve deeply enough within the self to commune with that self. Only by coming to terms with the boundaries of our own selfhood can we know what it means to enter the world of another. In our yearning for intimacy, we must take care not to push ourselves on another person and go where we are not welcome. We must control our desire to spend time with each other, so we can spend time with ourselves and be nourished from the divine spring that runs through us. A person who has not learned how to maintain his or her own boundaries of self will not know how to deal with these boundaries in another. True intimacy can exist only between mature individuals—people who know who they are and who do not try to find their identity in someone else.

Keeping the proper boundaries in an intimate relationship also means taking all of our other relationships as well as those of the other person into account. We are social by nature. For better or worse, each of us has been shaped by a vast network of private and social relationships. It is impossible for us to leave them behind or to pretend as though they did not exist. These relationships form a part of our history: we can never escape them; we carry them with us wherever we go.

Relationships bring with them responsibilities: in the family, at work, in the community. Intimate friends must respect those responsibilities and encourage each other to remain true to their situation in life. If they do not, then they must question if the relationship is honest and based on mutual respect. Intimacy that seeks to usurp the legitimate claims of others is not intimacy at all, but a selfish and self-serving substitute.

Finally, keeping the proper boundaries in a relationship means recognizing our mutual dependence on God. "I am the LORD your God...you shall have no other gods before me" (Ex 20:2). By believing in God, we affirm our creaturely status and accept our human limitations. This prevents us from assuming false pretensions about ourselves and/or others. When a relationship becomes intimate, there is always a temptation to squeeze more out of it than is humanly possible. We place unrealistic demands on the other person, because we have somehow allowed that person to take the place of God in our lives. We are called to have good, intimate friends. None of them, however, are capable of taking the place of God.

The best way to maintain this boundary of self in our relationships with others is for us to be rooted in a deep and intimate relationship with Jesus. We do this mainly through prayer, that is, by spending time with him, by sharing our deepest thoughts and feelings with him, simply being alone with him and resting in his presence. When we pray, we not only draw closer to God, but also gradually come to see that all genuine relationships tend toward the divine. When we draw closer to others in a deep, intimate way, we cannot help but come to a deeper knowledge of God in our lives. "For where two or three are gathered in my name, I am there among them" (Mt 18:20). God who dwells within us and in our midst, is the one who has made such intimate relationships possible.

DEGREES OF INTIMACY

We are called to enter into and maintain healthy, intimate relationships with ourselves, with others, and with God. Each of these builds on the other and manifests itself in varying degrees and different levels of intensity.

INITIAL ATTRACTION ∾ The lowest level is that of attraction. Two people are drawn to each other: they like each other's company and enjoy spending time with one another. This pull is not necessarily physical; it can involve an attraction of minds, of personalities, of spirits, of interests, or what have you. Here, intimacy focuses on what gives pleasure in a relationship. We know each other in and through our mutual attraction. Our level of trust is also determined by what gives us pleasure. The stronger the attraction, the stronger the trust—at least for the moment.

At this initial level of mere attraction, what draws us together prevents us from seeing ourselves as we really are. We idealize the other person and are blind to his or her imperfections. We share, at times even deeply, but more with an ideal construed by our minds than with the flesh-and-blood person before us.

DOUBT ∾ Genuine intimacy will eventually grow out of this initial state of euphoria and move to the level of doubt. At this stage, the idealized picture of the person we were initially attracted to begins to show some cracks. The imperfections that we pretended to ignore or did not even see now confront us with all of their pettiness and powers of repulsion. We begin to doubt the intimacy we share. We wonder if the relationship is truly mutual, if we really desire to be intimate. The person before us seems more like a stranger than a friend. We feel we do not know him or her. Part of us wants to run away or turn back the clock. We regret having shared what we did. We begin to be suspicious of the other. We guard our trust and now dispense it with care.

We now see that intimacy requires time for it to blossom and bear fruit. We are uncertain of how to proceed. A choice lies before us. Do we continue or withdraw? Commit ourselves or call it quits? This choice may be complicated by how the other person now perceives the relationship. Rarely do two people arrive at this critical moment together. The discrepancy in time can cause great pain, especially when, for whatever reason, the relationship gets stuck on a superficial level or winds up coming to an end.

COMMITMENT ∼ If the two people decide to stick it out, the relationship moves from doubt to commitment. This level of intimacy involves a conscious and clearly thought-out decision on the part of both parties. We choose to continue walking the road of intimacy despite the faults and weaknesses we have found in each other. In the early stages of this walk, our commitment needs to be constantly reinforced and expressed. As time passes on, however, and as the relationship deepens, the commitment gets internalized and does not need to be constantly shored up. Intimacy, at this stage, involves a great deal of "putting up" with each other. It requires patience and a willingness to live with another's imperfections and their willingness to live with ours.

The deeper our commitment to intimacy, the deeper is our level of trust. By committing ourselves to each other in this way, we get to know each other more deeply and share on levels we never before thought possible. In time, we either grow out of our imperfections or learn how to get around them. It may even happen that what we thought were imperfections or weaknesses in the other were actually unconscious projections of our own weaknesses. In this case, our commitment to intimacy becomes an instrument of conversion.

UNION ∼ When intimate relationships are healthy, they eventually move from commitment to union. This process involves an internalization that can best be described as an experience of mutual indwelling. In such relationships, each person resides in the other's heart and experiences a sense of peace in the knowledge of the other person's unconditional love.

This sense of union traverses time and space. It enables us to go about our work and our daily tasks with the knowledge that we are supported by another's loving regard. No matter where we go or what we are called upon to do, we know that we are not alone. We intuitively sense the other's ongoing support in our lives. We know that someone else believes in us and will go to great lengths to be there for us in our time of need.

The intimacy of union enables us to rest in another's love. It involves a close union of heart and mind. At times, it even enables us to sense the thoughts and needs of our friend even before they are articulated to us. It also helps us to gain a deeper understanding of what it means for someone to abide in us.

TRANSCENDENT INTIMACY ∼ The last degree of intimacy occurs when those involved seek to extend the love they share to those around them. We feel so secure in the union we share with one another that they no longer need to focus on it. The union of our hearts is so strong and intense that we are able to move our attention outward in an attempt to share with those around us what we have learned.

We move our intimacy outward by seeking to form other sound relationships and to help others walk with us along the way of union and commitment. In this expansive form of intimacy, we do not consider our relationship to be exclusive; rather we understand it to be intrinsically oriented toward others. We again become willing to travel again the same difficult road of intimacy with others whom we have not yet encountered. In the end, a relationship of intimacy transcends itself by opening itself up to others. It seeks to widen the circle of friendship which we share and to help others to understand and to experience intimacy in their lives as well.

These five degrees of intimacy represent a movement from infatuation, to suspicion, to commitment, to union, and to transcendence. This process is gradual and occurs, not out of necessity, but by the free choice of those involved. It can be found in all three types of relationships in our lives: with ourselves, with others, and with God. It is also highly unlikely that someone can progress in one such relationship (for example, with ourselves) without making progress in the other two (for example, with others and with God). We may not necessarily be conscious of this movement in our lives, but it is there nonetheless. Once the road to intimacy has been traveled on one dimension of our relationships, the others are usually not very far behind.

GROWING IN INTIMACY

It is possible to grow in intimacy and to fall out of intimacy. This ebb and flow is part of the human situation, at least as it is revealed in our present circumstances. If we look back on the many friendships in our lives, we can probably point to a number which moved forward for a time and then, for whatever reason, broke up or simply faded away. We may try to calm ourselves by insisting that these relationships were never truly intimate in the first place. If we are honest, however, we would have to admit that some of them *were* genuine and, were it not for our own inadvertence and lack of interest, some could have been salvaged.

It may also be that some people are meant to enter our lives, touch us (at times, deeply), and then walk out of our lives, never to be seen or heard of again. In such cases, we should be grateful for the gift they have given us at that particular moment of our earthly sojourn, but at the same time wonder why it was that they could join us only for such a small part of the way. Two people never stand still in their relationship. Either they are moving closer to each other in intimacy or they are moving apart. The same can be said with our relationships to ourselves and to God. We grow in intimacy by keeping the needs of the other person foremost in our minds. When we do this, we hold a safe and secure place for that person in our hearts and allow him or her the freedom to open up to us even more. Since intimacy demands reciprocity, the other person must be willing to do the same for us.

We move out of intimacy when either one of us starts to focus on his or her needs and on what he or she is getting out of the relationship. Once this happens, the relationship weakens and starts to fade. While we would like to think that it can never happen, experience suggests that even very close relationships can go awry. This possibility ends only in heaven when, seeing God face-to-face and with our hearts completely at rest, we will no longer have the capacity to fall out of friendship with ourselves, with those around us and, most importantly, with God.

Life is messy, and so are our relationships. At one time or another, most of them, the ones we really care about, have probably gone through a series of life-and-death cycles, moving forward and then backward and then forward again along the scale of intimacy. The key to understanding the health of any one relationship is not whether it has slipped back from time to time (for example, from union to commitment, to doubt), but that its status has deepened over the years. Such a judgment cannot be made by examining a single moment in the relationship, but by looking at it over a long period of time. The most important trait to look for in the relationship is its resiliency, that is, its capacity to withstand an ongoing series of cyclic life-and-death patterns. All else fades in comparison.

Conclusion

We all desire intimacy in our lives and will go to great lengths to find it. We long for it so much because, deep down inside, we sense that we were made for it. Call it what you will—an intuition, a natural conviction, a sense of destiny—we know that our lives would be very much the poorer without it. We may be able to survive our human sojourn without intimacy in our lives, but we will never thrive. With it, we deepen our knowledge of ourselves and receive a sense of belonging that carries us through difficult times. Without it, we drift through life without ever realizing our fullest potential.

The possibility for intimacy is always before us. Whether we experience it in our lives, however, depends on whether we are willing to put down our guard and take the risk of revealing ourselves as we truly are. That risk is painful, but well worth taking. If we refuse to cross the distances that separate us and venture into the unknown, we will never experience the joy of being known by another. If we have not the courage to open ourselves to those around us, we will never come to see ourselves as others see us. Something will always be missing from our lives, and we will spend a great deal of time and energy looking for it in the wrong places.

Intimacy is a gift to be accepted with gratitude and participated in with joy. It bids us to respond to our deepest intuitions about who we are. It beckons us to cross the distance that separates us and to maintain appropriate boundaries. It encourages us to advance along its varying degrees and to grow in the resiliency that will enable us to weather whatever obstacles come our way. Intimacy bears few (if any) regrets. As our relationships deepen, we find ourselves reaching out to others. Attraction, doubt, commitment, union, and transcendence mark the trails of our quiet sojourn through life. We see these levels of intimacy reflected within us, in our relationships with others, and in our relationship with God.

Even when we wander, they still help us find our way homeward.

SURVEYING YOUR SKILLS

1. Who are the people closest to you in your life? Do you feel that you share an intimate relationship with them? If so, how did these intimate relationships develop? What specific steps were taken by you to get there?

2. Do you keep the proper boundaries in your relationships? Do you allow your friends and family members enough space in their lives to be themselves and to blaze their own trail through life? Or are you possessive of them and afraid to share them with others?

3. Do you experience different levels of intimacy in your life? Are you more intimate with some people than others? Do you feel yourself growing in intimacy with some? Have you ever fallen out of intimacy with another person?

4. Do you have a close, intimate relationship with God? How do you foster that relationship of intimacy? Do you feel that relationship deepening? Becoming more shallow? What has God done to deepen the relationship? Do you experience God as an active partner in the relationship?

5. Do your intimate friendships help you in your relationships with other people? Do they help you to reach out to others? Do they enable you to be less self-conscious and more in tune with the needs of others? Do you experience intimacy as life-giving to others? Does it help you to forgive others?

7
SEEKING FORGIVENESS
~
THE SEVENTH STEP

...And you show us the way to extricate ourselves
from our sins: we should look more toward you
than toward our sins, should trust more in your
grace than we fear from our sins. For your forgiveness is more than merely a wiping away of our guilt;
it is fulfilled in seeing you, in the love which you
give us to pass on to our brothers. Where there was
sin, there is now no gaping void; rather, your face is
shining there: let us transmit this radiance to everyone around us.

Adrienne von Speyr[10]

*W*hile in the process of learning to walk, children
are strongly focused on the present. They cannot
remain fixated on past grievances. They may scold
their feet for not moving as they should or grimace at the rock
they just tripped over, but these reactions are usually short-
lived. Learning to walk is serious business, and children have
little time and energy for much else, least of all for harboring
personal grudges of whatever kind. Learning to walk by faith
is likewise a serious and time-consuming activity. Although it
is not easy to forgive those who have wronged us, doing so
frees us up and allows us to focus our energies on the step
before us.

THE DIFFICULTY WITH FORGIVENESS

For many of us, however, forgiveness is easier considered than effected. Letting go of the bitterness within us that poisons our relationships and prevents us from seeing the good in others is one of the most difficult tasks we will ever face in life.

When others hurt us, our natural reaction is to do the same to them. We inflict injury for injury, blow for blow. We want to exact vengeance down to the last ounce. We seek to recover our losses by taking what was taken from us: "life for life, eye for eye, tooth for tooth, hand for hand, foot for foot, burn for burn, wound for wound, stripe for stripe" (Ex 21:23–25). These are the sentiments which govern our thoughts and actions in our dealings with those who have hurt us. We want to hurt them back, no matter what the cost. We want to do unto them what they have done unto us. Our world seems to be driven by this primitive sense of judicial reckoning. We live our lives with a huge balance sheet in our minds, and we never forget what others have taken from us and owe us.

This way of thinking has become so deeply rooted in our lives that many of us are not even aware of it. We may paint a pretty picture of forgiveness and love of enemies, and so on, but our relationships with others tell a very different story. We ignore those who have slighted us. We harbor bitterness toward them, talk about them behind their backs, and devise complicated ways of paying them back in kind. If we feel any remorse, it is only that the world is not a kinder, gentler place. Since we cannot change it, we adopt its ways and survive as best we can. Tit for tat is the unspoken rule by which we live. The law of survival reigns: "Sink or swim," "Do or die'" "Eat or be eaten." We insulate ourselves from others. We always have our guard up. We are ready to pounce. Forgiveness makes little or no sense to us, possibly because we have never experienced it for ourselves.

WHY FORGIVE?

What place does forgiveness have in a world that is ruled by the clenched fist and the cold, impersonal stare? Why should we forgive others when they do not forgive us? What could it possibly accomplish? What benefit could we possibly accrue? We hear the words of Jesus: "Love your enemies and pray for those who persecute you" (Mt 5:44); Forgive "not seven times, but I tell you, seventy-seven times" (Mt 18:22). But these words have somehow lost their power over us. Perhaps they never had any. Perhaps we have heard them too many times. Perhaps we never really heard them in the first place. Besides, even if we did hear them, would we be able to put them into action? To utter them does not mean we can accomplish them, especially when we are smarting from a recently inflicted blow.

Pain often brings out the worst in us. When hurt, we can find ourselves acting in ways we thought we had long since outgrown. At such times, our deep, inner wounds rise to the surface and remind us of how small and petty we really are.

If we are to forgive, we must delve beneath Jesus' words and try to understand why this path was the one he chose to travel when he was among us. We must try and understand why he opted for the plowshare rather than the sword, why he became the Lamb of God and not God's devouring lion. If we are to follow his way, we must ask ourselves what he was trying to accomplish and why the way of forgiveness is a more human, and even more fruitful, way of life than the way of vengeance. Only by delving beneath Jesus' words and by struggling with the mystery they seek to reveal can we ever hope to fathom the mystery of what God promises to accomplish in us. Only then can we understand the meaning of his words and accept them in our hearts.

But how can we do this? How can we delve beneath his words? How can we understand the intent behind them? Jesus had many legitimate reasons to be angry with the world. He was looked upon with suspicion by the religious leaders of his people, betrayed by one of his closest followers, abandoned by most of his disciples, sneered at, scourged, mocked, and sentenced to die an ignoble death at the hands of an occupying Gentile army. Jesus ended his life on earth an outcast and a laughingstock of his people. His physical pains were but a faint reflection of the intense emotional and psychological suffering he was subjected to, especially by those who loved him the most.

Yet, in the midst of such excruciating pain, he somehow found enough strength at the end of his life to lift his head to heaven and utter these sincere and heartfelt words of pardon: "Father, forgive them; for they do not know what they are doing" (Lk 23:34). Jesus died forgiving each and every person who inflicted harm on him: those who plotted his death, those who crucified him, those who abandoned him, those who betrayed him. No one had even asked to be forgiven, yet still he forgave. His death on the cross gave authority to his words. Once we experience it in our hearts, his words cannot help but have power over us. The way of Jesus is the way of the cross is the way of forgiveness. We who call ourselves Christians must strive to follow in his steps.

THE WAY OF FORGIVENESS

What does it mean to forgive the way Jesus did? How do we go about praying for others as he prayed hanging from the cross? Are we even capable of such self-emptying action? Would we be able to utter the words—and mean them? From the heart? We will never know the answers to these questions if we remain locked up in an isolated world of bitterness and misplaced pride. To find the answers to these questions we must first look inside of ourselves and encounter there our own inner brokenness and need to be forgiven.

Only by asking the Lord himself to grant us forgiveness

will we ever understand the power that is locked up within the two simple phrases "I am sorry" and "I forgive." Only when we ourselves are freed from the burden of our sins can we experience the great sense of release and liberation that God extends to us through the power of the cross.

If we wish to discover the way of forgiveness, we need first to look within ourselves and walk the way of humility. We must recognize and admit the truth about ourselves. We must see how we really stand before God. We must admit our inner helplessness and inability to change ourselves. We must recognize that, left to ourselves, we cannot forgive the wrongs which others have perpetrated against us, let alone ask forgiveness for ourselves for the wrongs we have done—or even receive it. True forgiveness, the kind that comes from the heart, lies beyond our own meager powers of will. We cannot do it on our own. We need another's help. We need divine help, the help of God's grace.

If we ask God for forgiveness, we will not only receive it, but also find within ourselves the power to forgive. We will gradually find that there is no room in our hearts for any bitterness toward others. What hurt us so deeply seems insignificant when viewed against the backdrop of Christ's own suffering and willingness to forgive. We look upon our tormentors in a different light. We begin to show compassion for them as Christ showed compassion toward his own persecutors. Most of all, we see in our enemies a reflection of our own selves. We see in them our own ability to inflict pain and do damage to another's heart. We are able to forgive because we ourselves have been forgiven and we recognize the power that such an action brings to us.

If we refuse to forgive, we have not accepted the forgiveness of Christ in our own lives. If we refuse to forgive, we remain small and are unable to extend our horizons beyond our own inner hurts and groanings. We lose out on an opportunity to grow beyond our wounds and actually make the festering pains within us even worse. Bitterness feeds on bitterness. Wound feeds upon wound. If we are not careful, our isolation will increase to such an extent that all we will be able to see is our own pain, and all we will be able to feel is the bitterness and hatred that we bear toward others and, ultimately, toward ourselves. If we fail to walk the way of humility and then the way of forgiveness, we will ultimately find ourselves walking alone, in complete isolation from all warmth and genuine human contact.

The way of forgiveness calls us out of our festering wounds of isolation and self-hatred. It asks us to embrace God's love for us and to extend that embrace to others. It asks us only to ask for God's help in opening our hearts so that we will recognize how we have wronged ourselves, our neighbors, and our God. If we ask, the Lord will come; indeed, he already has come in our asking.

The way of forgiveness is the way of healing. We present ourselves to Jesus as did the many nameless people in the gospels who came to him and asked for healing of every sort of physical and spiritual disease. They came to him lame and blind, leprous and possessed, bedridden and paralyzed. They came to present their case to him, to touch his hand or even a piece of his garment. They came and none were ever refused. All were healed, each in his own time, as a way of showing forth the power and the glory of God.

We are all in search of forgiveness. We are all reluctant prodigals with no place else to return but home. We have wasted our inheritance on high living and superfluities. With nothing left in our purses, we turn back with our heads down low rehearsing in our minds what we will say when we present our case. We are sorry, but not necessarily for the best of motives. We have nowhere else to go and so now turn to God. We get down on our knees, but expect the worse. God has every right to be angry with us. We have not listened. We insisted on going our own way. We have strayed. And yet, in spite of all of this, we discover that God's love for us exceeds the demands of justice. God is compassionate toward us and rushes out to embrace us and does not stop to count the cost. God offers us forgiveness even before we get the chance to utter our own words of regret and sorrow. God welcomes us home as sons and daughters. We who were dead have come back to life. We who were lost are found (Lk 15:32).

STEPS TOWARD FORGIVENESS

With God's forgiveness and loving acceptance in our hearts, we are able to turn from the bitterness and hatred that enslave us and reach out to others with gentle and open concern.

- We do this first by asking God to help us to let go of the things that keep us from forgiving those who have wronged us and from seeking forgiveness from those we have wronged. Giving and receiving forgiveness are closely related and require a strong dose of humility to help us to see and accept the truth about ourselves. Neither can be accomplished without constant and heartfelt prayer. If we do not pray, we will never know how to give or receive a forgiving hand.

- In addition to prayer, we must look at ourselves and accept not only our smallness before God but also our utter inability to forgive the way we are asked to, that is, without reserve and without counting the cost. We must acknowledge God's hand at work in our lives. When we find ourselves ready and able to forgive we should attribute it not to ourselves but to the power of God's Spirit at work in our lives. The closer we are to God and the movement of the Spirit in our lives the easier will it be for us to forgive.

- Recognizing God's work in forgiveness does not mean that we are passive in the process that takes place. On the contrary, our active participation in the activity of God's grace in our lives is absolutely necessary. Without it, our forgiveness would not be truly our own; it would be God's and God's alone. But that is not how God has intended it to be. Grace works in us while allowing our normal faculties to function and perform their specific tasks. It works in us, not in spite of us. It accomplishes its task in and through our exercise of free will, not without it.

- There is always an element of risk involved when seeking or offering forgiveness. We must be prepared for rejection, but we should not allow the possibility of it to interfere with our efforts. We cannot control the way others will react to our sincere efforts to mend our differences and to heal the divisions between us. Through prayer, however, we can ask God to remove the bitterness in our own hearts and in the hearts of those who have hurt us or whom we ourselves have hurt. We must believe in the power of God to change people's lives and look forward to the day when both parties will be ready for healing to take place in their lives.

- As in physical healing, forgiveness often involves a long, gradual process. We are complex creatures. Bitterness and hatred coincide with the desire for forgiveness. The wound closes slowly. We must be careful not to rush the process, as if it is we and not God who are in control of it. We should also remember that deep wounds require more time to heal than surface wounds. For this reason, we need to be aware of the kind of wound we are dealing with. We also need to be patient with ourselves and with the other person. If we try to hasten the process too quickly, we may open the wound unintentionally.

- When physical wounds heal, they often leave a scar. The same is true for forgiveness. To forgive does not necessarily mean to forget. Our scars serve as reminders of what we have gone through. They bid us to learn from our past, especially our mistakes, and to appreciate even more the great miracle of healing that has taken place. Our scars can draw us together. When we look at them, we are reminded of where we have been, yet we can still raise our eyes in gratitude for what we have become. We look forward to the day when even the scars themselves will fade and reveal to us our deepest, truest selves.

- Forgiveness ends in gratitude. When two people are able to shed their bitterness toward each other and let go of their mutual suspicion, they can look back and marvel at the distance they have traveled. A broken relationship has been mended, and they recognize that it was not of their own doing. They rejoice in what has been accomplished in them, and they are grateful for being able to participate in a process that has borne such fruit.

We may or may not be aware of it, but all of us take these steps when we set out along the way of forgiveness. Some steps are more difficult than others. Some may seem almost impossible for us in the circumstances in which we find ourselves. Through it all, we must remember that the way of forgiveness is the path that was chosen by Jesus. He has walked before us and he now walks by our side. We may not see him or feel his presence. We may feel as though he has abandoned us or left us to fend for ourselves, but he is there. He carries us along the way of forgiveness. At times, he even shoulders our cross. He walks beside us, sometimes in our place, and helps us to utter from the heart with complete and utter sincerity the same words of forgiveness which he himself uttered so very long ago.

THE FRUITS OF FORGIVENESS

Forgiveness makes the world a gentler and more compassionate place. It brings out the best in us and helps us to see that we are not destined to be ruled by the dark forces that lie dormant in our souls. Forgiveness, in fact, is a sign of God's promise to us that we will one day overcome these dark forces. The fruit of forgiveness is living a life totally dedicated to God, that is, living a life in the Spirit. It is impossible to admit our faults, to express our sorrow, to make amends, and do away with bitterness and hatred, if we are not moved by the Spirit.

The spirit of the evil one is one of rancor and division; the Spirit of God is one of harmony and of peace. To walk the way of forgiveness, the path which Jesus himself followed, is to walk the way of the Spirit. That way enables us to live the ordinary events of our lives with extraordinary fervor and devotion. It helps us to put everything that happens to us into perspective and enables us to appreciate the great gifts that God has showered upon us.

The fruits of forgiveness are the fruits of the Spirit: "love, joy, peace, patience, kindness, generosity, faithfulness, gentleness, and self-control" (Gal 5:22). They come to us not of our own accord, but from the hand of God. They remind us that our lives are meant to be lived not for ourselves, but for others. And they remind us that our relationships with others have a strong effect on our inner lives. The Spirit cannot dwell within those who insist on harboring within their hearts the grudges of past injuries and unhealed wounds. It cannot come to those who prefer to ignore or, worse yet, actively taunt other people. It cannot move a heart that refuses to be moved, but chooses instead to live in fear and suspicion of other people.

Every time we hurt or are hurt we are confronted with a choice. We can choose the way of the Spirit or the way of hatred. The choice we make will have an effect not only on our relationship to other people, but also on our relationship to God and ourselves. The Spirit comes to us and offers us help in choosing love over hatred. The Spirit even prays within us, if we but open our hearts to its mild and gentle presence. The Spirit will do much for us, but it will not choose for us. It is we who must choose to cooperate with its quiet, transforming grace—or not. What we decide will say a great deal about who we are and where we are going in life.

CONCLUSION

It is difficult to forgive. To do so, we must put aside negative feelings, go outside of ourselves, and trust. The pain involved is sometimes excruciating, almost beyond what we can bear. We endure it not out of love for suffering, but because it is the way of Jesus, and it promises to transform us into more loving and compassionate human beings.

The way of Jesus is the way of the cross. It reminds us that we are able to forgive others only because God has first forgiven us. If we do not accept this way and make it an integral part of our lives, we will never know the full meaning of forgiveness from the heart. We will not know the full meaning of forgiveness because we will never have experienced for ourselves the deep satisfaction of being loved unconditionally and accepted as we are. Only when we open our hearts and allow God to bind our wounds and heal the broken areas of our lives will we understand the true meaning of forgiveness. Only when we have received the confidence and the assurance of being loved and deeply treasured will we risk the pain of rejection and ridicule.

Once we experience God's forgiveness in our lives, we find it easier to offer forgiveness to others. Suddenly, everything falls into place. We see what really matters and keep that foremost in our minds. Something is freed up inside of us and we are able to let go of the many hurts and insecurities that we can easily project outward on others. We find ourselves doing things we thought were beyond our capabilities. We reach out instead of keeping to ourselves. We learn to let go of our grudges and to deal with differences of opinion in healthy and constructive ways. We seek forgiveness from those we have wronged. We forgive those who have harmed us with an amazing gentleness and openness of heart.

All of this is possible because of our own experience of forgiveness in our lives. It is through forgiveness that Jesus lives in the members of his Body and they in him. It is through forgiveness that he suffers, dies, and rises in all who look to him and continue to trust in his promises.

SURVEYING YOUR SKILLS

1. Do you tend to bear grudges? Do you harbor bitterness in your heart when someone hurts you? If so, how does that bitterness manifest itself in your life? Can you see yourself ever letting go of that bitterness?

2. Do you find it difficult to forgive another person when he or she has hurt you? Do you find it difficult to ask for forgiveness when you yourself have hurt another? Which do you find more difficult: giving or receiving forgiveness? Do you think that the two are in any way related?

3. Can you think of anything right now that needs forgiveness in your life? With respect to yourself? To others? To God? What is holding you back from seeking that forgiveness? Is there anything you can do to remove that inhibition from your life?

4. Do you ask God to help you to forgive others? Do you ask God to help you receive forgiveness from them? Do you ask God for forgiveness for your own faults and failings? Does anything prevent you from turning to God at such times?

5. Do you bear any grudges against yourself? Are you able
   to forgive yourself for the mistakes you have made in your
   life? Are you harder on yourself than others are on you?
   Are you harder on yourself than even God is? If so, how
   does this prevent you from reaching out to others?

8

SERVING THE POOR

~

THE EIGHTH STEP

In giving us a mother's blessing, she admonished
us to live as Christians, to pray earnestly to God,
and above all else to strive to fulfill the most important of God's commandments: to love our neighbors and to feed and help Christ's needy brethren,
with simplicity and humility to raise our children
in the fear of God and to treat our servants as brothers. So we have lived here by ourselves these ten
years, trying our best to heed our mother's instruc-
tions. We have a guesthouse for the poor, where
there are more than ten crippled and needy people
in residence at the moment. Perhaps tomorrow we
will visit them.

The Way of a Pilgrim[11]

*T*he more children are able to walk, the more they
can do for themselves; the more they can do for
themselves, the more they can do for others. Walking by faith follows a similar rule of thumb. We cannot serve
others if we ourselves have no idea what walking in faith is all
about. If we try to separate one from the other, we will eventually find both ends coming up short. And that will get us nowhere.

The faces of the poor surround us and beg for attention.

They show us their pain and heartache. They open their shirts and reveal their wounds. They turn to us, gaze into our eyes, and look for solace. They cry out to us in pain and ask for shelter. We look at them and become restless. They make us uncomfortable. We would rather not deal with them. We wish to help them, but do not know what to do or where to begin. There are so many of them. Their pain is overwhelming. We feel helpless in the midst of their plight. We close our eyes and wish they would go away. We become angry when they do not. Why don't they leave us alone? Why don't they disappear? What do they want from us? Why do they disturb our peace?

The cry of the poor echoes down the corridors of our souls. Those who hear it cannot rest. The suffering of the poor shakes us out of our complacency. We cannot ignore them or pretend they do not exist. To do so would be to deny their humanness and do damage to our own. Their suffering touches us; their pain and sorrow stir within us. We must embrace them. We must enter into their plight and find our own within it.

The cry of the poor opens our hearts and moves us to action. What we do, however, must be done with care. We must not allow our actions to offend. We must be conscious of how we will be received. The poor do not want our pity, but our compassion. They do not want us to help them from a distance, but to be one with them in their plight. They do not want us to look down on them in their afflictions, but to share in their struggle for justice. That alone will lift their drooping spirits and restore their dignity. That alone will put them at rest and calm our troubled hearts.

THE GIFT OF THE POOR

"Truly I tell you, just as you did not do it to one of the least of these, you did not do it to me" (Mt 25:45). The poor are a gift to us from God. They reveal Christ in our midst and give us concrete opportunities to love him: when we feed them, quench their thirst, welcome them, clothe them, visit them when they are ill or in prison (Mt 25:31–46). Whatever we do to them we do to Christ. We have the words of Jesus to show for it.

We should not love the poor, however, simply because they lead us to God. Jesus proclaimed glad tidings to the poor because he loved them. He had no ulterior motive. To love them for any other reason (even a holy one) would be a subtle way of taking advantage of them. The poor have always been used as a means for another's ends. Christ came to stop this practice. He came "to proclaim release to the captives and recovery of sight to the blind, to let the oppressed go free" (Lk 4:18). His love was pure and unadulterated. He gave what he had and expected nothing in return.

To love the poor for their own sake means, first of all, stripping ourselves of any romantic ideas we may have of them. Given a choice, most poor people would opt for wealth. They would much rather not have to worry about finding work, paying the rent, putting enough food on the table, and keeping warm. If they had their way, they would have money enough to put an end to such worries.

Being poor does not necessarily make a person virtuous. Because of the way they have been treated, the poor often carry a lot of anger around with them. They also may have accumulated some bad habits. Drinking and drug use can be heavy; physical and verbal abuse, common; their families are often dysfunctional (and sometimes nonexistent). It is a terrible thing to be poor. Those who wish to love them must be prepared to suffer, not so much for their convictions, but for want of getting through to them. The poor tend to be suspicious of do-gooders, especially those from the middle and upper classes who are able to return to their homes in the suburbs after a day's work in the ghetto.

If the poor are difficult to love, then why are they such a

gift? This question does not have an obvious answer. To find it, we must experience their plight from within. Only then will we see how they put a mirror to our faces and help us to see our own inner poverty. Only then will we be able to fathom the extent of God's love for us. The poor do not have a monopoly on human pettiness and vice. They are just less devious than we are when it comes to hiding it. The poor put us in touch with our own limitations. In them, we see what it is like to be stripped of everything we hold so dear. In them, we see what it is like to be trapped by circumstances beyond our control. In them, we feel what it is to be ridiculed and looked down upon.

The poor are no different from us. In fact, they *are* us— and that is why they are a gift. In them, we come to understand God's special concern for us. He who emptied himself and took the form of a slave (Phil 2:7) has chosen to come to us and dwell among us (Jn 1:14). The cry of the poor is our cry, the cry of humanity. God has heard it and, in Jesus, has come to liberate us.

SOLIDARITY WITH THE POOR

To love the poor means to be in solidarity with them. We do so by identifying with their needs and concerns, so much so that we make them our own. When this occurs, we find ourselves always thinking about how we can alleviate their pain and make them more comfortable. To live in solidarity with the poor means to be in communion with them. To do this, we do not necessarily have to live with them, although, at times, we may have to. We must, however, be willing to take up their cause and follow through on our convictions.

We speak to the poor not primarily through our words, but through our actions. Jesus touched them, healed them, listened to them, encouraged them. And that is why they loved him. Jesus is the Word of God made *flesh*. He incarnated God's love and mercy for everyone he met—even his enemies. The poor are given many promises, but see so few of them fulfilled. They will listen to our words, but they will not believe them until they see some chance of these promises coming true.

Jesus was the fulfillment of God's promise to the poor. In him, God kept his Word to humanity. In his suffering and death, his plan of redemption moved from dream to reality. Jesus brought good news to the poor, and backed his words up with actions. His compassion came from deep within his heart and went out to all who suffer. In him, word and action were one. There was no discrepancy between what he said and what he did. That is why the poor loved him. He spoke (and acted) with an authority they had not seen for a long time.

"So shall my word be that goes out from my mouth; it shall not return to me empty" (Isa 55:11). Jesus dwelled in the world and now dwells in our hearts. He speaks the same words of good news to the poor that he did some two thousand years ago.

He now walks the earth through us. We are his eyes and his ears, his lips and his hands, his heart and his soul. We are the ones through whom he touches, heals, listens to, and encourages the poor. He lives in solidarity with the poor of this generation through our efforts to be with them, to commune with them, and to take up their cause. For this reason, it is very important that we ourselves be open to the presence of God in our lives. If we lose touch with this abiding presence, our actions in service of the poor will lose much (if not all) of their healing, liberating force.

WORKING FOR JUSTICE

Being in solidarity with the poor means working for justice. To champion their cause we must speak on their behalf and plead their case to anyone who will listen. The struggle of the poor is one of justice. They seek food, clothing, shelter, decent employment, all that is due them by virtue of their membership in the human family. They also seek the right to determine their future and the freedom to speak out against the injustices done to them.

The poor are constantly being taken advantage of, often in ways so subtle that they are not even aware of what is happening. Those who champion the cause of the poor try to make sure that this does not happen. The manner in which they do this will vary according to the circumstances they are in, the particular difficulties faced by the poor, and their own availability. For some, it will mean helping this particular person or family to get the education and training necessary to find decent work. For others, it may mean working in a particular community in order to raise the standard of the schools and social services. For still others, it may mean working on national and international levels to change unjust economic and societal structures that perpetuate the conditions of poverty. There are many ways in which a person can work for justice on behalf of the poor. One need only to take account of the situation, discern a viable response to it, and act accordingly.

Working for justice also means holding the poor accountable for their lives. The downward pull of poverty can have a detrimental effect on the way the poor view themselves. They are so used to being acted upon that they become passive in many other areas of their lives. When serving the poor, we must be careful that they do not develop a dependence on us. This would do nothing but shift the focus of the problem from one codependent relationship to another. The poor need to break out of this vicious cycle of dependency, if they are ever to lead normal and productive lives.

THE POOR IN OUR MIDST

The poor are not an abstraction, but real people with concrete problems that need practical solutions. If we are to live in solidarity with the poor and work on their behalf, if we are to champion their cause and strive to better their situation, we must open our eyes and become sensitive to their presence in our midst. This may sound easy to do, but it often is not, especially when we take into account the five dimensions of poverty in the world around us.

POVERTY'S PHYSICAL DIMENSION ~ The physical dimension of poverty is usually the easiest to spot. It is difficult not to be aware of a child who comes to school tired, hungry, and poorly clad or a family that suffers from unemployment and substandard housing. It is hard not to notice the struggle of a physically handicapped person as he or she attempts to cross the street or get on a bus or to see the hopeless gaze of a street person who looks to us for a handout as we pass by on the street. What to do? Alleviate their pain. But how? When dealing with the material needs of the poor, we must take care that their immediate needs do not block our awareness of their deeper, more fundamental wants. The goal here should be to meet their immediate needs, while at the same time working to solve the deeper social and medical issues that prevent them from leading fuller lives.

POVERTY'S INTELLECTUAL DIMENSION ~ There is also a mental or intellectual dimension of poverty. This level is often the cause of the material dimension of poverty. When it is alleviated, the physical needs of a person or group often fall into place. This is where education becomes so important in helping the poor to rise out of their need. When people are given the training they need to hold down good-paying jobs, when the standards of their schools are such that they can concentrate on their studies and get a good education that will help them to make valuable contributions to society, when community programs are instituted that give people a sense of pride in their cultural heritage, they become motivated, self-actualizing citizens who become part of the solution of society's ills.

POVERTY'S EMOTIONAL DIMENSION ~ There is also an emotional dimension of poverty. In this case, people are out of touch with their feelings and end up acting out in ways that are harmful to their own well-being and that of others. Emotional intelligence, as it is commonly referred to today, has a great deal to do with how a person functions in a group. Success in the work force, performance in school, and peace in the family are often connected to the level of emotional stability a person has in his or her life. By integrating one's emotions into his or her life, a person unburdens himself or herself of the unruly effects of passion and is able to relate to others in a calmer, more peaceful manner. The more a person gets in touch with his or her feelings, understands them, and tames them, the more will he or she be a competent and productive member of society.

POVERTY'S SOCIAL DIMENSION ~ Closely related to the emotional dimension of poverty is the social. We have already seen how the emotions have an effect on the way in which a person functions in a group—for good or for ill. It is also true that society can produce structures that deliberately perpetuate a servile underclass for purposes of economic or social ends. It is usually the superior attitude of the rich and powerful that keeps such structures in place. In these instances, the oppressed classes suffer from a number of physical, intellectual, emotional, social, and even spiritual handicaps. To liberate them, drastic measures are often required. The oppressor must be called to task, and many basic, fundamental ways of organizing the social and economic structures of society rethought.

POVERTY'S SPIRITUAL DIMENSION ∾ Finally, there is a spiritual dimension of poverty. This kind of poverty cuts across class and economic barriers. On a material level, a person can be rich or poor and still be spiritually wealthy or impoverished. The roots of spiritual poverty go deep within a person's soul and touches on his or her entire attitude toward life. The measure of a person's spiritual well-being is the depth of his or her relationship with God and the extent to which he or she reaches out to others in need. The most generous people around are often those with the least material wealth at their disposal, while the stingiest have often the most economic means. Spiritual poverty is something a person chooses in the depths of his or her heart. One rises out of it, however, not through one's own efforts, but by being docile to the movement of the Spirit and responding to the call to conversion.

In laying out these various dimensions of human want, we must be careful not to narrow our understanding of poverty to one of them or think that some are more important than others. An understanding of poverty, for example, that focuses exclusively on material needs will be blind to much of the psychological stress that arises from the social stigma of being associated with a cultural underclass. Similarly, an exaggerated emphasis on spiritual poverty may blind us to the very real material needs of those we wish to serve.

The most effective strategies against poverty have been those that take a broad, interdisciplinary approach to the problem. The multidimensional nature of human existence demands a similar approach to the war against poverty. Poverty must not be overly materialized *or* spiritualized. It must be faced head-on and looked at squarely, keenly evaluated, and dealt with on a practical basis.

Poverty is a complex reality and embraces many levels of human existence. Because these dimensions are intimately related to each other, one rarely encounters a situation in which only one aspect of poverty is at work. One normally feeds on another, influences a third, and then a fourth, and so on. For this reason, care must be taken not to take a naive stance toward the problem.

Poverty is a universal human phenomenon, but is also intimately connected to the historical circumstances in which it is found. It is tied not just to the obvious expressions of physical want, but involves a vast array of intellectual, emotional, social, and spiritual needs. To overlook these equally valid and, in many cases, more painful expressions of human misery is to miss the full extent to which poverty has lodged itself in human experience.

CONCLUSION

The cry of the poor is comprised of a cacophony of discordant tones rising from various dimensions of human existence. In some places of the world, this ugly sound of human beings in misery rises to such a ferocious pitch that it prevents us from appreciating the goodness and beauty in life. It is at this point that total impoverishment sets in.

He or she is truly poor who, despite the tragedies encountered in life, cannot relish whatever joys and blessings that happen along the way: "Two thieves looked out from prison bars; one saw mud; the other, stars." The irony is that such a state of impoverishment is found just as frequently among the well-to-do as among the materially poor—perhaps more frequently.

Appearances hide as much as they reveal. We need to see beneath them and recognize all that enslaves us. At times, the cry of the poor can only be heard once we unmask the illusions and self-deceptions that we mistake for the truth about ourselves. Only when we do this can we hear the cry of our own inner poverty and reach out to others with a tender, compassionate heart.

Solidarity with the poor begins with the recognition of our own inner poverty and ends in that communion with God made possible by Christ's passion and death on the cross. As members of Christ's Body, we share in the plight of the poor in a special way. Christ, who embraced the lot of the poor in his Incarnation and paschal mystery, now shares that embrace with us in his resurrected, Mystical Body. The struggle for solidarity has thus been made holy by his blood and divinized by his Spirit. It has become an action of the Word of God in which we, as members of his Body, now actively partake.

"Blessed are you who are poor, for yours is the kingdom of God" (Lk 6:20). In one way or another, all of us share in the plight of the poor. Jesus' message was not just for a select group, but for all people. His message of freedom was directed toward all human beings, regardless of their position in life, wealth (or lack thereof), or social stature.

"You always have the poor with you…" (Mt 26:11). The obvious literal intent of Jesus' words should not obscure the spiritual significance which they convey. The poor will be with us always, because we carry them within us. We are the poor. The entire spiritual life can be summed up as the journey by which we come to a deep and deeper recognition of this one central truth of our lives.

Those of us who are further along in this journey are asked to look back and help the others along, one step at a time, until the laggards can walk with surer steps. By helping them to carry their crosses—whatever they may be—we make Christ present both to them and to ourselves.

SURVEYING YOUR SKILLS

1. What does solidarity with the poor mean to you? Sharing their plight? Working to alleviate their pain? Helping them to help themselves? Is it a feeling of compassion for them

that motivates you? An intellectual appreciation of them?
A commitment to serve them?

2. Are the poor responsible for the situations in which they
   find themselves? Should they be left to fend for themselves?
   Are they being taken advantage of? In what ways? What
   kind of help should they receive?

3. Who are the poor in your midst? In what concrete ways
   do you manifest your solidarity with them? In what concrete ways do you work on their behalf? Can you think of
   anything more you could do for them?

4. Do you consider yourself poor? If so, in what way? Which
   dimensions of poverty have touched your own life experience? The physical? The intellectual? The emotional? The
   social? The spiritual?

5. What does the poverty of Jesus tell you of God's commitment to the poor? Do you believe that God is with them in
   a special way? If so, why? What can the poor tell us about
   ourselves and our relationship to God?

9
LONGING FOR GOD
~
THE NINTH STEP

O immeasurably tender love! Who would not be
set afire with such love? What heart could keep from
breaking? You, deep well of charity, it seems you
are so madly in love with your creatures that you
could not live without us! Yet you are our God,
and have no need of us. Your greatness is no greater
for our well-being, nor are you harmed by any harm
that comes to us, for you are supreme eternal Goodness. What could move you to such mercy? Neither
duty nor any need you have of us (we are sinful and
wicked debtors)—but only love!

Catherine of Siena, *The Dialogue*[12]

*D*esire is what propels children into walking. Without this deep-seated longing to transcend their
present limitations, they would never strive to extend themselves and thus never come to enjoy one of the great
pleasures of life.

Desire is also what moves us along in our walk of faith.
Our yearning for God rises up within us at the first moment of
our existence and never leaves us, not even after death.
Throughout our lives we are conscious of this longing in varying degrees and with changing intensities. Sometimes it is very
prominent in our thoughts; at other times, it is barely recog-

nizable, hidden as it is in the onrush of life's daily concerns. For the most part, the intensity of our desire falls somewhere in the middle, changing ever so slightly as our image of God silently takes shape within us and comes to light.

This longing for God accompanies us at every stage of our human journey. In the womb, it moves us into the labors of birth and the challenges of growth; in life, it propels us into the decisions that shape who it is we are and who we deeply desire to be; in death, it moves us past the limitations of human knowledge and into the mystery of our divine origins.

This longing for God is pure and utter gift. It comes from God and has its destiny in God. It is a vestige of God left in the deepest recesses of our hearts to remind us of where we came from and where we are called to return. This trace of the divine lingers within us. It stays with us all during our waking hours and even while we sleep. It is God's way of telling us that we are never alone and that we will never be left to fend completely for ourselves. It is God's way of telling us that, even now, we are being drawn into intimate contact with the ground of our being and that all we need to do is allow ourselves to be led by our deepest yearnings.

LETTING GO

Many of us are, unfortunately, out of touch with these deep yearnings of the heart. For one reason or another, we feel threatened by the longing for the divine within us and choose to cover it over with false, artificial remedies. We fill our lives with useless diversions that keep us from confronting our deepest, truest selves. In doing so, we run away from ourselves and evade God's call in our lives. We distance ourselves from the very voices within us that speak to us of God. We forget where we have come from and look elsewhere for the truth that gives us life.

The result of this distancing and distraction is that we

rarely go beneath the appearances of things and wind up dwelling on the surface of life. Once there, we often mistake the comforts of life for life itself and somehow convince ourselves that life really has little much else to offer. The tragedy of it all is that we then go about living our lives settling for less when deep down inside we instinctively know that there is so very much more to be had.

When we fail to journey beneath the surface of life, we cannot come to a deep and penetrating knowledge of ourselves. We measure ourselves instead by acquired externals such as power, wealth, honors, success, and other people's opinions of us. When these and similar concerns become the meaning of our existence and define for us the basis of our entire self-worth, they become false, disingenuous idols which must be confronted, cast down, and expediently done away with. Their hold over us needs to be broken; their roots must be pulled out of the unturned soil of our souls. Only then will we be free to experience God in the depths of our hearts; only then will our deepest yearnings rise to the surface and invite us to set out on a journey of discovery of our deepest selves wherein rests the quiet stillness of the divine.

It is difficult to let go of the things that bind us and hold sway over us. They rarely let go of us without a struggle. They are often so deeply rooted in us that we cannot do much more than voice our desire to be free of them and invoke God's help to overcome them. For most of us, letting go means getting out of the way and simply letting God in. It means recognizing our own inability to change our lives and asking God to help us. By consciously turning to God in prayer and by asking for the assistance we so desperately need but cannot give to ourselves, we find that the inner yearnings of our hearts will gradually find their way to the surface. Once there, these yearnings will confront the darkness and root out whatever holds sway in our lives that is not of God.

For many of us, finding God means letting go of our

desire to be in control of our destiny. It means opening up our hearts so that we will be able to encounter ourselves "at depth" and learn that the inner longings of our hearts are the means through which the transforming grace of God enters our lives. By giving up control of our lives, we allow our inner yearnings to rise to the surface and permeate every aspect of our lives.

These yearnings ache within us and accompany us in all we do. They tell us of God and of the divine yearning to be with us. They show us how to listen to the voice of our own spirit and to find there the dwelling place of God. Our yearnings for God are God's way of drawing us toward the Holy Spirit.

Through these yearnings, our human hearts find rest in the divine heart. In them, God's Spirit comes to us, yearns along with us, dwells with us, and provides us with a deeper appreciation of the mystery of life and death. We who yearn with God are promised that we will one day rest in God. And it is in the yearning, the longing and the groaning, the living and the dying, that the resting has already begun.

THE GIFT OF SOLITUDE

One way of releasing the false attachments in our lives is by cultivating the gift of solitude. We do this by gradually removing ourselves from the things that bind us and by putting in their place the knowledge and experience of our utter aloneness with God. Such purposeful displacement, even if it be for a short while, is our way of bringing to the fore the relative value of the things we cling to. By putting some time aside each day in order to seek God in the quiet of our hearts, we give our spirits the time they need to breathe in the divine silence. Without such times in our lives, we cannot distinguish the wheat from the tares, let alone the kernel from the chaff. Everything gets mixed together, and we can easily lose our perspective on what really matters.

Solitude itself is a gift from God. It means being alone so that we can have a deeper sense of God's presence in our lives. It is not simple "aloneness;" nor is solitude always practiced in separation from others. To be sure, some of us may be capable of being alone for long periods of time (and may even enjoy it), without ever having a sense of God's deep, abiding presence. At the same time, others of us may be able to live in quiet, solitary peace, while leading very busy and productive lives.

Solitude is more a state of mind than a matter of physical separation from people and worldly activities. This state of mind is a gift of God and is based on the *belief* that God communes with us in the quiet of our hearts, the *hope* that this communion of hearts will ripen over time, and the *love* that God pours into our hearts and, from there, into the lives of others.

The deeper our solitude, the deeper our faith, hope, and love. The deeper our solitude, the more will we be detached from everything that gets in the way of our relationship with God. The deeper our solitude, the less likely will we need to rely on *feeling* the presence of God in our lives and the more readily we are willing to *trust* in the abiding presence of the divine within us. The deeper our solitude, the less will we have need of the external framework of solitude (that is, separation from the world, retreat from worldly activity, and so on) and the more we will be able to interiorize it so that we can embrace those we encounter in a spirit of humble service.

Lives dedicated to solitude and service do complement rather than contradict each other; each is oriented toward the other and is invigorated by its relationship to that other. Our activity in the world loses its vitality when it is cut off from the quiet and prayerful search for God in the interior reaches of the soul. Similarly, our solitude becomes needlessly introverted when it cuts itself off from the love of those who surround it.

Solitude leads to service; service leads to solitude. When this close circular relationship is broken, we open ourselves up to the forces of self-aggrandizement and self-deception. Service keeps us from making an idol out of solitude and the quest for interior peace—and solitude keeps us from making an obsession of service. When separated from each other or unduly dichotomized in our lives, the twin tools of service and solitude exert undue pressure on us to live the demands of the gospel by our efforts alone. When integrated in our lives, they unleash the power of the Spirit and enable us to do even the most ordinary of tasks with an extraordinary reverence for the simplicity and holiness of life.

HOLY SIMPLICITY

Together, solitude and service manifest themselves in a life of holy simplicity. "You shall love the Lord your God with all your heart, and with all your soul, and with all your strength, and with all your mind, and your neighbor as yourself" (Lk 10:27). Solitude keeps a person focused on God alone; service keeps one focused on the love of neighbor. Together, they keep a person's attention on all that really matters in life. All else recedes to the background as the person's life becomes more and more consumed by gospel values.

To live a life of holy simplicity is to lead the life of a saint. As the saints draw closer and closer to God, they not only grow in holiness, but also share in the divine simplicity. God, the source of all holiness, is also utterly simple: God's truth is God's goodness is God's unity is God's beauty. These transcendental values subsist in God without complexity and division. In a similar fashion, the saints exude a fundamental simplicity in their lives which increasingly manifests these same fundamental values to others. That is not to say that they *become* God in the literal sense of the term, but only that they powerfully manifest the life of God in the concrete circumstances of their lives.

"God became human so that we might become divine."[13]

These words of Saint Athanasius remind us of the divinizing scope of God's redemptive plan. Holy simplicity is one of the concrete manifestations that this process of divinization is taking root in our lives. It means accepting God's love for us with the innocence of a little child and trusting that, whatever happens, God always has our well-being and best interest at heart.

"Truly I tell you, unless you change and become like children, you will never enter the kingdom of heaven" (Mt 18:3). God became a child so that we might become childlike in our relationship with God. Childlike innocence does not mean that we are to be naive or impractical in our relationships and daily affairs, but only that we have become increasingly marked by a deepening sense of trust in God's providential care. It means that our lives of solitude and service have become so intertwined that, like the saints themselves, we are able to discern the face of God in those we serve and find our neighbors' hearts nestled with ours in the heart of the Lord.

To lead a life of holy simplicity is to walk in the footsteps of Christ. Jesus is the man of solitude, the man of service, the man of childlike and holy simplicity par excellence. In him there is no discrepancy between divine and human. His humanity was divinized by his own divinity and bathed in the light of Spirit imparted to him by "Abba," his Father.

The Incarnation is the concrete expression of this divine simplicity. Through it, God chose "to be with us" literally—in the flesh. Of the many thousands of ways in which God could have come to us, the Incarnation is surely the simplest, the most straightforward, and most childlike. God became a child before becoming a man. His birth, his growth, his life, his death all reveal that holy desire on God's part to draw all of human experience to the divine heart and to be present to it in a way never before imagined.

Because of the Word made flesh, God understands human experience from within. From that moment on, Jesus would now accompany us in our journey through life. He is with us in the darkness of our mother's womb and at the moment of our birth. He walks beside us in our childhood and adolescent years; he is there as we grow to maturity, feeling the weight of responsibility and the demands that life brings to us. He is there in all our pain and sorrow, in our tears and in our grieving, in our suffering, in our dying, and especially in our death. He is there also in all the good times, in our experiences of family and friends, in our work and in our play, in the food we eat, in our sleep, in our dreams, in our romances, our loves, and in all the joy and laughter, hope and excitement that the adventure of life carries our way.

Through Jesus, God has entered our human story—and made it his own. As a result, God now holds out for us the opportunity to enter into the divine story, that is, enter into the eternal generation and procession of Love who, in utter simplicity, manifests itself in the threefold relationship of Father, Son, and Spirit.

This participation in the divine life is the purpose and goal of human existence. We are made by God to be transformed by God, to gaze and be gazed upon in the intimacy of Love who is God. Jesus, the Word made flesh, is mediator of our divine becoming. Because of him, we are able to enter into the mystery of the divine intimacy. With him we are entitled to call God "Abba," our Father. Through him and in his Spirit we are able to turn to God at all times, in every situation, regardless of the place, time, or circumstance.

PRAYING ALWAYS

To live in holy simplicity is to live a life of constant prayer. That is not to say that we spend all of our time in chapel, or that we neglect our daily chores and duties to spend time alone with God in the privacy of our rooms. It does not even mean that we are consciously aware that we are praying to God when we are doing so. It means only that we live our lives in communion with the Spirit and that we allow ourselves the freedom to be led by it in all the events of the day.

When we participate in the divine life, everything we do is taken up into it and becomes a heartfelt prayer to God. In childlike simplicity, we are able to trust that God's hand is upon our shoulder in each and every circumstance. Our thoughts naturally turn to God in gratitude for everything that comes our way. We feel free to talk to God with our lips, in our thoughts, with others, especially with our friends, and in our hearts.

Since each of us has a unique relationship to God, it follows that "praying always" will manifest itself in different ways, depending on our personalities, our situation in life, and the circumstances we encounter from one moment to the next. Each of us will express in our lives a different rhythm of prayer involving our bodies, our emotions, our minds, our spirits, and our community. Each of these five dimensions of human existence is important and should not be neglected in our ongoing communion with God.

Because of the subtle differences in our makeup, however, each of us will express these dimensions in different mixtures and combinations that make each of our days uniquely our own when turning to God. Those of us who feel more at ease with the physical dimension will give glory and praise to God through vocal prayer and song, through the work of our hands, and by fast and abstinence. Those of us who feel more at ease with the emotional dimension will try to name our emotions, own them, and share them honestly with God. Those of us who feel more at ease with the mental dimension will turn to God more frequently through spiritual reading, meditation, and journal writing. Those more at home on the level of the spirit will turn to God more frequently in the quiet of their hearts' contemplation and through centering prayer. Those more at home with the social dimension will commune with God more readily praying with others in a prayer group or at liturgy. Whatever our own individual leanings, it is important for our spiritual well-being that we try to integrate each of these aspects—the physical, the emotional, the mental, the spiritual, and the social—into our daily rhythm of prayer.

To pray always means that at every moment of our day at least one of these dimensions will be at work in our communion with God and will have a beneficial effect on every other aspect of who we are. The challenge of praying always is ultimately the lifelong task of finding that particular rhythm of prayer that best suits us in our daily circumstances. It also entails a willingness to nurture those aspects of our being with which we feel most uncomfortable and to turn them over to God. In doing so, we allow God to commune more deeply with us; we, in turn, are able to delve more deeply into the mystery of God's love for us.

When viewed in this light, the liturgy of holy Mass becomes that time when, gathered as the one Body of Christ, the Church gives expression to each of these dimensions of our human makeup. When we gather for Eucharist, we genuflect and bow, sing and pray vocally to highlight the physical dimension of our existence. We allow our emotions to settle down and be moved as we put time aside for them to be with the Lord. We listen to and expound the sacred Scriptures in order to nurture our minds with the Word of God. We sit in silence to allow our spirits to commune with the Spirit of God. We do all of these things together to highlight our common humanity and to affirm our oneness in Christ.

In the liturgy of the Eucharist, we allow every aspect of our beings to give praise and glory to God. We do all of this with Christ, who shares these dimensions with us and who joins us in the Holy Spirit in our prayer to the Father. Every celebration of the liturgy should take each of these dimensions of our existence into account when we pray to God. It should do so not only because these dimensions represent important facets of who *we* are, but because they are dimensions of

Christ's human makeup. The Eucharist is, first and foremost, an action of Christ. In it, we join Christ as members of his Body in raising his heart and mind, his feelings and emotions, his body, his soul, and his spirit—along with our own—in one consummate act of living praise.

CONCLUSION

Our yearning to be with God is given to us by God to remind us of our divine origins and destiny. That yearning can be numbed, however, by our tendency to lose ourselves in the pursuit of external rewards and comforts. For this reason we must find a way of letting go of the things that weigh us down and keep us from growing in our relationship with God. The practice of solitude is one such way of removing ourselves gradually from all creaturely attachments.

Solitude offers assistance by helping us to put our lives in perspective and by helping us to discern the relatively unimportant nature of everything that gets in the way of our relationship with God.

Solitude naturally leads to service; service, to solitude. Together they lead us along the path of holy simplicity, a path already marked for us by Jesus, the Word of God made flesh.

By becoming human, God gathers all of human experience into the Divine Self. In thus making the human story a divine story, God extends to each of us an invitation to share in the mystery of divine life. Through this participation, we are able to commune with God and to pray without ceasing. We do so especially by finding the right rhythm of prayer that, at any particular time of our lives, best enables us to offer our bodies, our emotions, our minds, our spirits, and our community in humble praise and adoration to God.

The Eucharist should provide space for each dimension of our existence to open itself up to God. This action of Christ carries us along and seeks to pour itself out into the rest of our lives. The injunction to pray always is thus intimately tied to our celebration of the eucharistic liturgy, which is for us the source and summit of Christian life.

Letting go, the gift of solitude, holy simplicity, and praying always—the way before us has already been traveled by Christ. His life is a perfect example of someone who let go of the things that kept him from God, who sought God in solitude, who offered himself in humble service to humanity, who led a life of holy and childlike simplicity, and whose communion with God led him to pray at all times and without ceasing. As his disciples, we join him side by side in that yearning for God that began at the moment of our birth and which will end only when we confront what lies beyond the veil of death. Until that time, we continue to walk the way of discipleship, seeking God in all things and trying to nurture our intimacy with Christ with all our heart, mind, soul, and strength.

Surveying Your Skills

1. Do you sometimes feel as though you are living only on the surface of life? Can you identify anything specific that you need to let go of? What keeps you from experiencing life at its depth? What helps you to do so?

2. Do you enjoy being alone? Can you spend time with yourself and discover who you are beneath all the false appearances? Can you listen to your heart? Do you understand what your heart is saying to you? Can you give expression to those thoughts?

3. Do you feel a deep yearning in your heart to be with God? Do you sense God's presence in your life? What is that presence like? Is it different from the yearning? Or is it closely connected to it? Does God speak to you in your yearning? What is God trying to say?

4. Do you lead a simple life? What value does a life of simplicity hold for the spiritual life? Do you see a relationship between holiness and simplicity? What is it? What concrete steps can you take to lead a simpler life? What effects will these steps have on your relationship to Jesus? What will they tell others of your hopes and dreams?

5. Do you look upon prayer as a gift from God? Is prayer something that you do on your own? Does God play any role in it? What does it mean to pray always? Have you ever experienced this sense of deep, abiding prayer? What can you do to deepen your experience of communion with God?

10
LIVING IN HOPE
~
THE LAST STEP

Life is hope free from all anxiety, wealth hidden from the senses but attested by the understanding and by the true nature of things. Farmers work laboriously, sowing and planting, sailors endure many dangers, and children learn reading and writing and other branches of knowledge. They all look forward with hope, laboring with joy. Outwardly they sacrifice immediate advantages, but in reality, even if they forfeit what they sacrifice, through their patient endurance they gain what is of far greater value.

Peter of Damaskos, *Twenty-Four Discourses*, VI[14]

Children learn to walk in order to have greater freedom of movement. That is what they hope for, even if they do not have the mental capacity to conceive of the idea and express it as such. Without that freedom, their options in life will be greatly curtailed, sometimes drastically so.

In like manner, learning to walk by faith is not an end in itself, but a means toward even greater goals. To live in hope is to keep those goals firmly in focus. Hope is a mental disposition that helps us to look at the present in light of a future promise. With it, we are able to accept imperfection and look forward to the day when imperfection will fade from the scene of human consciousness. Without hope, we can sink into despondency and self-pity, regretting the way life has treated us and seeing little possibility for the fulfillment of our dreams.

Hope helps us to accept the limitations we encounter by enabling us to see beyond them. It causes us to live in the present, while recognizing that the present is itself moving forward toward its own completion in God.

Hope is never static. It moves with us as we journey through life, adjusting its horizons as often as we adjust our sight and shifting directions as we adapt to the dangerous and rugged terrain before us. It keeps us focused on our final goal and makes that goal present to us in the very midst of its absence.

Hope changes as we change, lighting our way in the darkness just enough so that we can find sure footing for our next feeble and uncertain steps. It moves as we move, extending itself always just a bit before us so that we are able to see the possibilities of the present moment. Hope extends the present into the future. It swells within us and helps us to see that time itself is a swelling and longs to break out of its current historical flow.

LOOKING FOR HOPE

We live in a world desperately searching for hope. People everywhere are looking for something that will open up life's meaning to them. Without hope, life grows stale and loses its sense of purpose. We move aimlessly about from day to day and from year to year with little or no sense of where we are going. To offset this lack of direction in our lives, we grab hold of all kinds of passing fads and fashions, expecting to find something that will fix our gaze and carry us through the rest of our sojourn through life.

Sometimes we come upon something—an idea in a book, a person we have met, a cause we are drawn to—that seems to fit just right. We focus on this discovery and understand ourselves in light of it. We live by it and are consumed by it. We concentrate all of our energies on it and allow it to guide our decisions. Such an expression of hope is quite natural to us and can be found almost anywhere and in anything: in our work and hobbies, in our plans and possessions, in our schools and institutions, to name but a few.

It is worthwhile to invest our hearts in such a discovery and find hope in such basic human goods—but this diversion can also be very dangerous. If we are not careful, these same goods can take control of us and divert us from what really matters. This occurs because these diversions tell us little of the deeper questions of human existence; they fail to satisfy our deepest longings; they disappoint us even as we enjoy them.

There is another kind of hope, however—one that lies beyond our own meager capacity for good. We cannot devise it or program it; nor can we limit it and dispense it at will. It is a gift from God, one that builds on our natural ability, but also goes far beyond it. This hope enables us to do everything in life in concert with the love of God. It swells up within us and ignites in us a deep yearning to be with God and to rest in the presence of the Spirit. It makes us look forward to the time when time itself will be transformed, and we will enjoy a continuous, abiding vision of God's innermost nature. It eagerly awaits the establishment of the kingdom proclaimed by Jesus and made possible by the events of Calvary.

HOPE IN JESUS

This hope changes everything in our lives. It helps us to see Jesus as someone who will lead us through the valleys and pitfalls of life. It gives us a deep, personal trust in him and makes us willing to follow him even when the path he has marked out for us seems strange and uncertain.

To hope in Jesus means to be guided by the cross—which, for us, is now inseparable from his person. It means to believe that the Christ event did indeed happen and will also happen to us. It means affirming deep in our hearts that the way of the cross leads to the empty tomb and to the viewing of the Resurrection as *the* pivotal event of our lives.

It would not make any sense if we say we place our hope in Jesus, yet do nothing to foster our relationship with him. To turn to him only in emergencies or at the last moment of our life on earth is to miss the whole point of what God wants for us. Jesus has come to us to make it possible for us to go to God. He entered our world, gave of himself to us completely, became our nourishment and source of our hope so that in and through our relationship with him we could journey together to the Father. Jesus represents God's hope for us and our hope in God. He has come to us to show us that our deepest and innermost dreams are not only possible, but have already become a reality. He asks us only to trust him and to follow him with our hearts.

We cannot do this, however, if we never attempt to get to know him. We do this as we would if we were getting to know any other person: by talking to him, by sharing our dreams with him, by taking walks with him, by listening to him, by playing with him, by eating and drinking with him. If Jesus is as important to us as we say he is, it should be evident to others that we know him and have spent time with him. Otherwise, all that we say about him will be nothing but lip service to an ideal in the guise of a person who has no real impact (or relevance) for our present experience.

ENKINDLING HOPE

People today desperately long for something to hope in. They have lost their bearings and feel as though they are drifting aimlessly about in a world that offers them little to look forward to or anticipate. Everything around tells them to live for themselves and to garner as much pleasure and power, as many possessions, as they can while they can, because there is nothing else worth having, nothing more to the lives they live, nothing more to life itself.

Such pleasures, however, cannot fill the great void within their hearts. They cannot satiate their deep yearning for transcendence or the desire for something permanent in life, something that will not fade away with the passing of time, something that will carry their hearts beyond the pale of death.

Dissatisfied with the prospects before them, many have journeyed near the brink of despair. They peer over the edge, stare into the abyss, and see nothing to keep them from falling in. Some of them actually do. We can recognize them by the cold, listless look in their eyes and by their sad, fatalistic view of life. We do not have to go far to find them. Some of them are our friends and neighbors, perhaps even members of our own families. Some of them belong to our churches and even worship beside us in the same pew. These people have somehow lost hope. They yearn for what they have lost or possibly never had, and look for someone who will rekindle the flame from the tinder of anxiety and pain that has taken its place.

What can we do to help? What part can we play in bringing about a badly needed change of heart for these hopeless people? How can we rekindle the flame of hope within them or start it up again with renewed strength and vigor? There is no routine or mathematical formula that will necessarily work in every case. There are, however, a number of things that should be kept in mind in our dealings with such people.

RECOGNIZE OUR LIMITATIONS ~ In the first place, we must be able to recognize the limitations of what we can and cannot do. If our own hope is a gift from the Lord, what makes us think *we* can give it to others? It is God who enlivens people's lives with hope. The most important thing we can do is to pray for these people, asking God to bless them and to draw them closer to him.

It is likely that the hope we presently share is the direct

result of people who have actively and tirelessly kept us in prayer before God. Should we not do the same for others? "If in my name you ask me for anything, I will do it" (Jn 14:14). As members of Christ's Body we are in a unique position to lift others up to the Lord in prayer. We must be careful not the shirk the important responsibility we have to pray for others in need.

DEEPEN OUR OWN HOPE ～ Next, we ourselves must continue to be men and women of hope. Recognizing where this gift comes from, we should be grateful to the Lord for working in our lives and for blessing us with this new way of looking at the world. The best way we can show our gratitude to God is by rejoicing in our hope and by allowing this gift to permeate more and more of our daily activities. As hope deepens in us, we find ourselves increasingly able and willing to be instruments of God's love in the world. This means that we become more and more open to the movement of the Spirit in our lives and ready to reach out to others at appropriate times and circumstances.

HOPE THROUGH CHRIST'S BODY ～ When we reach out to others at such times, it is important for us to be aware that we do so not as isolated individuals, but as members of Christ's Body. We reach out, in other words, not just with our own meager gifts and talents, but with the support of countless individuals who are all mysteriously united by their faith in Christ. We reach out to others with the firm conviction that Christ himself is reaching out through us—that Christ, this day, uses his members to reach those who do not yet know him or who need to know him better. For this reason, it is very important that, when reaching out to others, we ask the Lord to help us to move out of the way of the action of the Spirit, to allow it to work through us and, if necessary, even in spite of us.

HOPE THROUGH FRIENDSHIP ～ When we reach out to others, we must allow them to be themselves. We gain nothing by trying to push ourselves or God on someone when they are not ready (or able) to hear. We must be ourselves and allow others to be themselves. This means walking beside them, listening to their stories, their complaints, their pain, their troubles. We show others we care for them by allowing them to air their thoughts in a safe, nonthreatening atmosphere. We must seek to establish a bond with those we wish to help and trust that through that bond the Spirit will work in its own quiet way. The flame of hope is kindled in a person's heart more through gentleness and patient listening than by anything else. Very often it is the bond of friendship that we establish with another person that will make the difference in his or her life and be the key factor in giving that person a lasting experience of hope.

HOPE THROUGH SHARING THE TRUTH ~ Still, when the time comes and the other person seems ready to listen, it is important for us to speak the truth about ourselves and what we hope for. We should not hide the importance of our relationship with Jesus in our lives. Nor should we be embarrassed about it or feel as though we must explain it away. "Is a lamp brought in to be put under the bushel basket, or under the bed, and not on the lampstand?" (Mk 4:21). When the time comes, we must be eager to share with others the source of hope.

This sharing can be done directly or indirectly, publicly or privately, in word or in gesture. How we do it is not as important as that we do it, although even here it is important that we take circumstances and personality into account. We are limited only by the confines of our own imagination. The possibilities for genuine sharing of our hopes are endless.

To be a source of hope for another is a great privilege, one we should not take lightly. For this to happen, we must turn to the Lord in prayer and ask that our own hope be strengthened and continually renewed. Only in this way will we be able to get out of the way and allow the Spirit to do its work. Only in this way will our own hope continue to shape itself according to our needs and lead us further along our journey homeward.

CONCLUSION

We hope in God because of all that God has done for us in Christ. That hope is real and living, not an abstract concept or a distant, far-off reality with little or no significance for our lives. It makes a difference in our lives; it is deep in our hearts and evident in our words, thoughts, and actions.

Jesus is no further away than the nearest person. How we act toward that person is how we act toward Christ. Our welcome, our care, our service, our love are all signs of Jesus' presence in our midst and of his kingdom that is already here and will one day manifest itself in all its glory.

To live in hope means that we look upon all the imperfections that we encounter in life—within ourselves, in other people, in society, in the Church—as subject to the gentle, transforming grace of God. It means that we are patient with those who have these imperfections, that we suffer whatever inconveniences they cause in our lives, and that we are able to look beyond them. It also means that we are able to envision a world without them, a place where these imperfections have been first purified and then gradually transformed by the presence of God in the depths of the human heart.

Finally, to hope in God means that the forces of shadow and night no longer have a stranglehold over us. The light of God's Spirit penetrates even the darkest and remotest caverns of our hearts and gradually casts out whatever evil and negative forces it finds in us. With the Spirit dwelling within us, even our prayer comes alive with a deep yearning for the kingdom that is to come. The Spirit groans within our hearts as we eagerly await the coming of the Lord. That groaning is itself a sign of the kingdom's presence in our midst. It is God longing in us and with us for the fullness of time, when everything will be in God and when we will finally see God face-to-face.

SURVEYING YOUR SKILLS

1. What does it mean to live in hope? What does it mean to live in despair? How does a person of hope deal with the difficult times in life? How have *you* dealt with the difficult times in life? Have you learned from your past mistakes? If you could, what would you now do differently?

2. Do you think of yourself as a person of hope? What makes you think that way? Would others describe you in the same way? Have you experienced different levels or degrees of hope in your life? If so, what caused them? How did you move from one level to another?

3. Do you feel you have enkindled hope in others? If so, how? Have you ever been an obstacle to a person's journey in hope? If so, what would you now do differently? Do you pray for those whose lives you have affected? Do you ask them to pray for you?

4. Do you experience hope primarily as an individual or does the experience of hope have a communal value for you? Does the hope of Christ's Body, the Church, have an impact on your daily life? If so, in what way? If not, why not?

5. Does hope come from you or from God? Is it natural? Supernatural? A mixture of both? What does it mean to say that Jesus is the source of your hope? Do you hope in your own resurrection? Do you hope one day to see God face-to-face? What does the end of your journey hold for you?

BREATHING OUT
(A Prayer)

Be with me, Lord.
Watch over me.
Guide me.
Move me.

STEP BY STEP
(A Poem)

Step by step
We travel,
Learning,
Discerning,
Burning within,
Testing the ground
Before us,
Taking the risk
Of stumbling,
And falling,
And losing our way.

Step by step
We travel,
Moment by moment,
Breath by breath,
Need by need,
Prayer by prayer;
Seeking God
In all things,
In all times
In all places,
In all circumstances.

Step by step
We travel,
Walking by faith,
And by doubt,
Living in hope,
And in fear,
Seeking to grasp
What we cannot see,
Or hear,
Or touch,
Or understand.

NOTES

1. Alphonsus Liguori, *Prayer, The Great Means of Obtaining Salvation and All the Graces Which We Desire of God,* in *The Complete Works,* ed. Eugene Grimm, vol. 3 (New York: Redemptorist Fathers, 1886–94; reprint ed., Brooklyn/St. Louis/Toronto: Redemptorist Fathers, 1927), 49.
2. *The Collected Works of Teresa of Ávila,* vol. 3, trans. Kieran Kavanaugh and Otilio Rodriguez (Washington, D.C.: ICS Publications, 1985), 386.
3. Jean-Pierre de Caussade, *Abandonment to Divine Providence* (Garden City, N.Y.: Image Books, 1966), 46.
4. For the corresponding faces of faith (i.e., intellectual, fiducial, and performative), see Avery Dulles, "The Meaning of Faith in Relationship to Justice," in *The Faith That Does Justice: Examining the Christian Sources for Social Change,* ed. John C. Haughey (New York: Paulist Press, 1977), 14, 23, 34, 39.
5. Thomas à Kempis, *The Imitation of Christ,* ed. Harold C. Gardiner (Garden City, N.Y.: Image Books, 1955), 131.
6. *The Confessions of St. Augustine,* trans., John K. Ryan (Garden City, N.Y.: Image Books, 1960), 246–47.
7. Cited in *The Philokalia,* vol. 2, trans., G. E. H. Palmer, Philip Sherrard, and Kallistos Ware (London/Boston: Father and Faber, 1981), 158.
8. Athanasius of Alexandria, *De incarnatione,* SC 199:458–59; PG 25:191–92.
9. Thomas Merton, *No Man Is An Island* (Garden City, N.Y.: Image Books, 1967), 130.
10. Hans Urs von Balthasar, *First Glance at Adrienne von Speyr,* trans. Antje Lawry and Sergia Englund (San Francisco: Ignatius Press, 1981), 232.
11. *The Way of the Pilgrim,* trans. Olga Savin (Boston and London: Shambhala Pocket Classics, 1991), 109–10.
12. Catherine of Siena, *The Dialogue,* trans. Suzanne Noffke (Mahwah, N.J.: Paulist Press, 1980), 275.
13. See above Chap. 2 n. 2.
14. Cited in *The Philokalia,* vol. 3, trans. G.E.H. Palmer, Philip Sherrard, and Kallistos Ware (London/Boston: Faber and Faber, 1984), 224–25.